CREATIVE CAKE DECORATING

Rose Cantrell

WEATHERVANE
BOOKS

Contents

introduction

Welcome to the creative world of cake baking and cake decorating. No other form of art expression can be as rewarding as creating a masterpiece of design that can be enjoyed by the senses of sight, smell, and taste.

Throughout the pages of this book you will find cake and cake-decorating ideas for the novice as well as for the skilled baker. In creating these cake designs no special equipment or ingredients were used that cannot be purchased in a large department store or five and dime. The majority of the designs can be made with your present kitchen equipment.

Most of the decorating ideas in this book can be adapted to any flavor of cake. Where no cake recipe is included, you can use your own favorite recipe or cake mix—just be sure the cake is the size called for in the recipe given here.

Unfortunately, many cooks think of cake decorating as being difficult and time-consuming. Others, of course, delight in the creativity and in the beauty of the finished piece of art. Most of the attractive designs in this book are not difficult to make. Try them—enjoy the beauty of your accomplishment. You will soon find that you are also creating "masterpieces" of your own.

helpful hints to successful cake baking

In order for your decorated masterpiece to turn out as you desire, you must start with the proper foundation: the cake.

The following pointers will be helpful in making a proper foundation.

1) Read the cake recipe completely before beginning, to determine if you have the proper ingredients and equipment to make the cake.

2) If you are using a cake mix, it is still vital to read the directions carefully. Mixing speeds and the order of the addition of the ingredients should be followed precisely to obtain the desired result.

3) Be sure you use the proper pan size. Too large a pan will make the cake layers flat and shrunken-looking. Too small a pan will cause the batter to run over the sides of the pan and form a hard crust on the outer rim of the pan.

4) Your pan should be made of the right type of material. A bright pan of lightweight metal is the best type to use.

If your baking dishes are glass, be sure to reduce the baking temperature by 25°F.

5) Prepare your pans for butter cakes by greasing and flouring the insides of your cake pans before beginning to mix your cake.

Pans are not greased for sponge cakes or angel-food cakes. My mother always keeps separate pans for her sponge cakes and angel-food cakes. Angel-food cakes will not rise properly if grease is present in the pan, and the oil present in the sponge cake tends to leave a grease film on the pan in which it is baked.

6) Preheat your oven for 10 minutes before baking your cake. To save energy and still remember to preheat your oven, first assemble all your ingredients; then

turn on your oven; finally, mix your cake. Most cakes take no more than 10 minutes to measure and mix.

7) All ovens are not regulated the same. Therefore, about 5 minutes before the stated baking time has expired, test your cake for doneness by inserting a toothpick in the center of each layer. If the toothpick comes out clean, your cake is done.

8) If you are layering your cake, and the layers have baked unevenly, even the layers by using small marshmallows to raise the height of the layers in selected positions.

9) If the recipe calls for the cake to be split into one or more pieces, you can obtain even split layers by measuring the distance to be cut and marking the measured distance at intervals with toothpicks. Use these toothpicks as your cutting guide.

10) A cake must be completely cooled before frosting. If it is not cooled, it will melt the frosting.

frostings and icings

Four basic types of frostings are used to decorate cakes in this book. Each has its own unique features that dictate its decorating use. Therefore, the different types of frostings cannot be interchanged among recipes without affecting the results.

The characteristics of the frostings used in this book are:

1) Sugar–water frosting—This is commonly referred to as icing or glaze. The frosting combines powdered sugar and a liquid. It is easy to spread, and, when the proportion of liquid increases, the mixture becomes pourable.

2) Uncooked butter frosting—A quick frosting that is almost fail-proof if you remember to sift the sugar to prevent lumps. This frosting is very easy to color and flavor.

3) Cooked frosting—This frosting is a little more difficult to make, but it offers a long-lasting frosting. It is made by cooking milk with granulated sugar and then thickening with powdered sugar.

4) Boiled frosting—This frosting is made by cooking a sugar syrup until just the right consistency and then beating in egg whites.

Success depends on having all ingredients at room temperature and cooking the frosting the exact time specified in each recipe.

planning the decoration

There are three basic areas to consider when planning the decoration of a cake:

1) Top—As a general rule, this is the area of the cake that will be the focal point of the decoration. It will set the theme and color scheme for the cake. Thus, it should be designed and decorated first. The remaining areas should harmonize in color and design with this area.

2) Sides—The decoration of this area is planned so as not to detract from the focal point of the cake. It will generally consist of the same topping used to cover the top of the cake (see Candy Cake page 71); but can be an integral part of the design as well. (see Violet Garden page 93)

3) Border—The border is used to connect the sides and top of the cake. Often this area is of the same topping as the sides (see Spring Garden page 22) or can be decorated to add an accent in design and/or color. (see Orange Rosette Cake page 128)

equipment needed

A few basic pieces of equipment are needed in order to make the decorative designs in the whipped cream, meringue or icing decorated cakes you find in this book. You will be able to find this equipment in any large department store in your area. Pictured on the next page is an intermediate kit for decorating cakes that contains all of the necessary tools needed for you to turn out beautiful masterpieces.

1) Greaseproof paper for lining pans and making icing bags.

2) Regular icing turntable or you can make your own by placing a flat plate over a large mixing bowl.

3) Straight edge for making straight lines. A metal ruler will also work.

4) Spatula for spreading frosting. A spatula works better than a table knife because it has a larger and more pliable spreading surface; therefore makes smoother strokes.

5) Deluxe professional icing turntable. A luxury for the serious cake decorator.

6) Metal tubes or tips—Special shaped metal open-end tubes that are used to create the designs with whipped cream, meringue or icing. The tubes fit through the small end of the icing bag or fasten to the end by the use of a coupler. A coupler is a device that fits through the bottom end of the icing bag which enables you to use the same icing bag for more than one tube.

The six basic tubes are:
- a) Round Tube—used for writing, dots, piping and outlining
- b) Leaf Tube—used for leaves, trim flowers, decorative cake borders
- c) Rosette or Star Tube—used for stars, rosettes, fleur-de-lis, scrolls, shells
- d) Flower—used for making drop flowers
- e) Rose Tube—used for roses, sweet peas and ribbons
- f) Basketweave—used for basketweave design, ribbed strips, serrated edges

7) Flower pins used for piping icing flowers.

8) Column stands for tiered cakes. (not essential)

9) Icing bags which come in canvas, plastic, or can be easily made from greaseproof paper. (see pages 7 and 8)

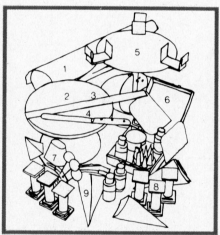

How to make
a paper icing bag

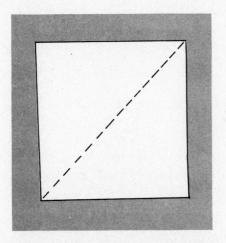

Cut 8-, 10- or 12-inch squares from thick greaseproof paper and cut the squares into triangles.

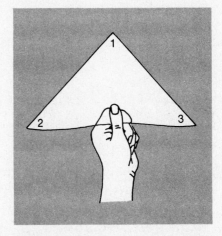

Hold the triangle in your left hand with your thumb in the middle of the longest side.

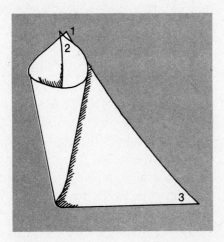

Make a sort of cone by bringing point 2 up to point 1 and hold with your right hand.

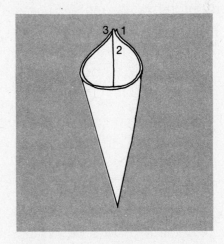

Bring point 3 around the cone with your left hand and hold it behind 1 and 2 with right hand.

7

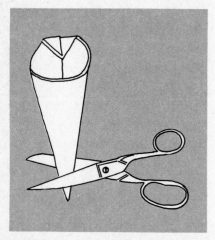
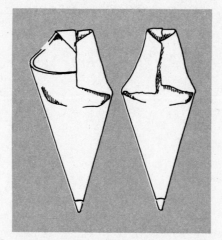
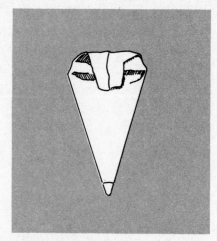

Fold down the point to hold the bag together, and cut off the tip, a little at a time until the tube fits securely.

Drop in a decorating tube and half fill the bag with icing. Fold the two sides in towards the middle.

Fold the top down to seal in icing. Now you may decorate.

practicing the techniques

After familiarizing yourself with the equipment used in cake decorating, you are now ready to begin practicing the techniques of cake decorating.

Pressure—In order to form the exact decoration you wish to create, you will need to develop the feel of pressure on the icing bag. The less pressure you use, the thinner your line will be and the more delicate the details. The more pressure you use, the thicker the line and the less detailing. (Pictures A and B on opposite page)

Rhythm—To create a flowing balanced design, you must learn to move in steady continuous movements. To assist you in developing rhythm, you may want to draw simple designs on waxed paper and practice following these lines. (Picture C on opposite page)

Position—The position in which you hold your icing bag will also help you develop rhythm and balanced designs.

If the desired results are flowing continuous lines (Picture A on opposite page) you will need to hold the icing bag at a 45-degree angle a fraction above the surface to be decorated. This position will allow the icing to fall on to the surface and not be pressed into the surface medium.

If the desired results are stationary designs that require a build-up of frosting (Picture B on opposite page), you will need to hold the tube straight up and down while touching the surface lightly with the icing tubes to press the design into the decorated surface. As you make the stationary design, slowly raise the icing bag to taper the design.

Once you have mastered the techniques of pressure, rhythm, and angle, practice different designs by varying the tubes you use. (Picture D on opposite page) You are now ready to create your first masterpiece. Why not try Birthday Layers on page 107 or Orange Rosette Cake on page 128.

8

A

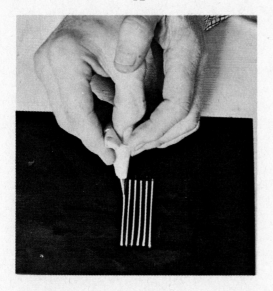

1) *Light pressure—thin lines*
2) *Tube held at a slant to form a continuous flowing line*

B

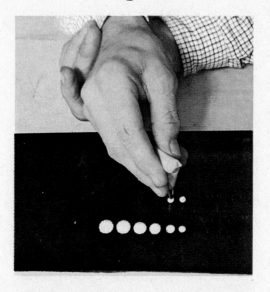

1) *Varying degrees of pressure to obtain different sizes of rosettes*
2) *Holding tube upright to anchor drop decorations such as flowers or leaves*

C

Rhythm—Uniform even design

D

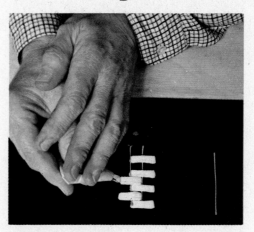

Using two tubes to make a basket-weave design. The round tube is used to make the stave and the serrated tube used to make the basket-weave portion.

piping a flower

Now that you have learned how to decorate a cake using the basic cake decorating equipment, you are ready to advance to ornaments such as piped flowers.

Piped flowers are made by taking a flower pin (Picture E), dabbing a small amount of icing on the pin and covering it with a square of waxed paper.

Place flower tube in icing bag and fill with icing. The flower is formed by squeezing the icing bag with one hand while rotating the pin with the other hand.

Steps in Piping a Flower (Picture F)

1) Pipe a bud in the center of the pin.
2) Encase the bud with petals by moving up, around and downward. Overlap each petal sightly with the one preceeding it. As you pipe the flower, rotate the pin counterclockwise.
3) Remove flower from pin and allow to dry completely before storing in an air-tight container until ready for use.

E

Flower pins used to pipe flowers

F

Various stages in piping a rose

G

Various ways to arrange the petals of piped flowers

alternative decorations

Although the most popular form of cake decorating is icing, other mediums can be used to create beautiful cakes.

Natural foods such as nuts, sugar and fruits make simple, yet elegant, cake decorations. (see Walnut Spice Cake page 26)

creating with marzipan

If you are an artist who prefers to create with your hands, then marzipan is for you. This medium resembles clay and you mold your decorations as if you were forming a clay pot.

You can buy marzipan already made or make it yourself using one of the following recipes:

marzipan #1

2½ cups blanched almonds
1 pound powdered sugar, sifted
twice

2 egg whites
1 teaspoon vanilla

Place almonds in a food processor and grind until they are fine and mealy. Remove almonds from processor and combine with powdered sugar in a large bowl. Work with pastry blender until well-mixed.

Beat the egg whites with a fork until slightly frothy. Add ½ of the beaten egg whites to the almond mixture and mix to a paste. Add the vanilla, mixing thoroughly. Add enough of the remaining egg whites to make the mixture the consistency of pie pastry.

Place on a cold surface and knead as with bread dough until it is smooth.

marzipan #2

1 8-ounce can almond paste
1 egg white

Place the almond paste in a mixing bowl and work with a wooden spoon until creamy. Add 1 teaspoon egg white and mix until combined, adding more egg white if needed.

Turn out on a cold surface covered with powdered sugar and knead until smooth.

Note: To color marzipan, add a small amount of coloring at a time. Knead to mix thoroughly before adding more color.

molding the marzipan

While working with marzipan, you will need plastic wrap to keep the marzipan covered to prevent it from drying out, a bowl of flour to dust your hands to prevent the marzipan from sticking, and cold water to moisten petals so they will stick together.

A rose is a beautiful and easy flower to form from marzipan.

1) Using a piece of marzipan about the size of a walnut, form the bud and molding base for the flower. (Picture H on opposite page)

2) Form the blunt-base rose petals by flattening a piece of marzipan, about the size of a cherry, paper thin. Hold the marzipan in the floured palm of one hand and flatten it paper thin with the thumb of the other hand. (Picture I on opposite page)

3) Fasten the two blunt-base rose petals onto the bud, one at a time, overlapping the two petals slightly. (Picture J on opposite page)

4) Work with the petals until they form a pointed center. (Picture K on opposite page)

5) Form each outer petal one at a time in the same fashion as you did the blunt-based petals. To fasten, baste with cold water and mold bottom of petal to base. Work outer edge of petal to a paper thin thickness, flaring the petals out as you work. (Picture L on page 14)

6) Cut off base and place flower on a lightly-floured surface to dry.

Now that you have mastered the art of molding with marzipan, why not try the Bridal Basket page 133, the Thanksgiving Cake page 117, or the Vegetable-Garden Cake page 74.

H

Forming the bud and base of the rose

I

Forming the blunt-based rose petals

J

Fastening the blunt-based rose petals onto the bud

K

Forming a point from the blunt-based rose petals

L

Molding outer petal to blunt-based petals

garnishing with chocolate

For the chocolate lover, beautiful decorations can be made from liquified chocolate chips. To liquify chocolate chips, place the chips over a double boiler and soften. (about 8 minutes)

When chips are softened, vigorously beat until they liquify. (Picture M on opposite page)

Chocolate Curls—To form chocolate curls, pour melted chocolate chips onto a chilled marble slab or a kitchen counter chilled by using a bag of crushed ice. Spread chocolate to about ⅛ inch thick; let harden until chocolate loses its gloss. (approximately 2 hours)

Using a long, slender knife, form curls by holding the knife at a slight angle and pulling it across the surface of the chocolate. (Picture N on opposite page) (see Lincoln Log Cake page 110)

Free Form Chocolate—Make an icing bag out of greaseproof paper. Cut a small hole in the end of the icing bag. Fill bag with melted chocolate chips. Slowly squeeze chocolate through icing bag onto a piece of waxed paper, forming design as you go along. Chill. (Picture O on opposite page) Lift the chilled designs from the waxed paper and garnish cake. Dimension can be given to your design by placing the design on mounds of frosting or whipped cream. (Picture P on opposite page) (see Dragon Fly Cake page 108)

Chocolate Leaves—Place melted chocolate chips in a shallow bowl. Wash leaves. Pull a leaf, upside down, over the surface of the melted chocolate. (Picture Q on page 16) Remove any excess chocolate from leaf by tapping it against the side of the bowl. Place leaves, chocolate side up, in refrigerator and allow to harden. (Picture R on page 16)

When the chocolate has hardened on the leaves peel off the leaves. Use to decorate cakes such as Chocolate Rose Dream page 124)

Enjoy . . .

M

Melted chocolate chips

N

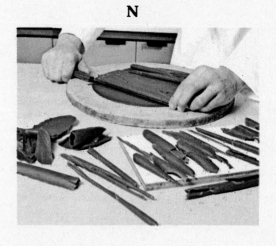

Making chocolate curls

O

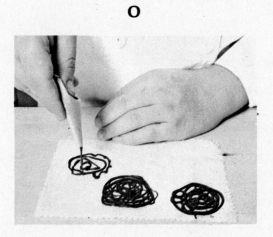

Making free-form chocolate designs

P

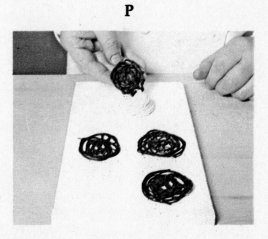

Removing free-form chocolate design from paper and supporting with frosting mounds

Q

Coating with chocolate leaf

R

Removing leaf from chocolate and removing excess chocolate

S

Removing leaf from chilled chocolate

nut cakes and toppings

almond jelly layers

For a change, frost a cake with nuts.

Yield: 12 servings

2¼ cups cake flour
1½ cups granulated sugar
4 teaspoons baking powder
1 teaspoon salt
½ cup shortening
1 cup milk

1 teaspoon vanilla
2 eggs
2 cups currant jelly, room
   temperature
2 cups chopped almonds

Combine flour, sugar, baking powder, and salt. Add shortening, ¾ cup milk, and vanilla to dry mixture. Beat on low speed for 2 minutes. Add eggs and remaining milk. Continue to beat for an additional 2 minutes.

Grease and flour 3 8-inch cake pans. Divide batter evenly among the pans. Bake cake in a 350°F oven for 20 minutes or until done. Remove from pans and cool.

Whip jelly until spreadable. Spread jelly between layers; stack layers. Cover sides of cake with a thin coat of jelly; cover sides with 1 cup almonds before jelly sets. Pour remaining jelly on top of cake; cover top evenly. Spread remaining almonds around the edge of the cake and in a circular design in the center of the cake, as illustrated. Allow jelly to set before serving.

almond jelly layers

almond wreath

almond wreath

Yield: 12 servings

¼ cup warm water
1 package active dry yeast
½ cup milk
½ cup granulated sugar
½ teaspoon salt

¼ cup margarine
2 eggs, beaten
2½ cups unbleached white flour
1 teaspoon cinnamon
¼ cup blanched whole almonds

Measure warm water into large bowl; sprinkle in yeast. Stir until dissolved.

Scald milk. Stir in sugar, salt, and margarine. Cool to lukewarm; add to yeast mixture. Beat in eggs, flour, and cinnamon, and beat for 5 minutes. Cover. Let rise until doubled in bulk.

Grease and flour a 1½-quart tube mold. Arrange almonds in bottom of mold.

Stir down batter; beat vigorously for 3 minutes. Pour batter into prepared mold; let rise until doubled in bulk.

Bake cake in a 350°F oven 1 hour or until done. Let rest in pan 5 minutes before removing. Serve cake warm.

babka

A delicious Polish cake.

Yield: 12 servings

½ cup milk
⅓ cup shortening
1 teaspoon salt
¼ cup granulated sugar
1 package active dry yeast
¼ cup warm water
2 eggs
½ teaspoon dried lemon peel
2¼ cups all-purpose flour
1 cup raisins
¼ cup chopped almonds

Scald milk. Add shortening, salt, and sugar; stir until melted. Cool to lukewarm.

Add yeast to water; stir until dissolved. Add to cooled milk mixture; mix well.

Beat eggs; add with lemon peel to milk mixture. Add flour; beat until smooth. Cover; let rise about 6 hours.

Punch down. Add raisins; beat until smooth and elastic.

Generously grease a brioche pan; sprinkle the bottom with almonds. Pour dough into pan. Let rise, uncovered, about 20 minutes.

Bake babka in a 425°F oven 20 minutes. Unmold immediately.

babka

spaceship cake

spaceship cake

A delightful cake for your space-age fan.

Yield: 10 servings

1 1-layer chocolate cake mix	**2 cups chocolate chips**
2 cups slivered almonds	**2½ cups hot-fudge sauce (can be**
5 tablespoons hot water	**used in place of last 4**
½ cup light corn syrup	**ingredients above)**
¼ cup margarine, melted	

Prepare cake mix as directed. Pour batter into long, shallow loaf pan. Bake cake at 350°F for 20 minutes or until done. Cool slightly before removing from pan.

Place cake on cake rack, top-side-down. With a sharp knife, cut off sharp corners of cake.

Stick almonds into cake in a staggered row design, as illustrated. Cover to prevent drying.

Combine hot water, corn syrup, and margarine in top of a double boiler. Bring mixture to a boil; continue to boil until margarine melts. Remove from heat; stir in chocolate chips. Beat until sauce is combined. (Or, heat hot-fudge sauce over a double boiler until it drips from a spoon.)

Cool sauce to warm; spoon *slowly* over cake with almonds. (This process must be done slowly to allow the sauce time to adhere to the nuts and cake.) Allow sauce to set before serving.

almond strawberry tower

Yield: 12 servings

1 prepared 10-inch angel-food
tube cake
¼ cup drained pureed frozen
strawberries
3 cups whipped topping
1 cup toasted almonds
1 cup whole strawberries

Cut a round piece of plastic from a milk jug; place it over the hole in the center of the angel-food cake. Cover cake to prevent it from drying out.

Fold pureed strawberries into whipped topping. Frost sides and top of cake with strawberry whipped topping.

Cover cake with almonds, pressing slightly with the palm of your hand to adhere almonds to whipped topping.

Arrange strawberries on top of cake. Refrigerate.

spring garden

Yield: 11 servings

1 9-inch white-cake layer
¼ cup cherry jam
3 cups powdered sugar, sifted
¼ cup water, approximately
55 whole almonds
11 candied cherry halves
11 citron strips

Using a sharp knife or a string, cut cake layer into two parts. Spread jam between layers; stack.

Sift powdered sugar into a mixing bowl. Add water until an easy-spreading icing forms. Cover top and sides of cake with icing.

Form flowers on top of cake by using almonds to form the flower petals, cherries to form the centers, and citron strips to form the stems.

Allow icing to set before serving.

tropical-isle cake

The topping gives the decorative touch to this unusual cake.

Yield: 2 dozen servings

¾ cup liquid brown sugar
½ cup margarine
½ cup all-purpose white flour
½ cup whole-wheat flour
2 eggs, beaten
1 teaspoon vanilla
1 tablespoon all-purpose white flour
½ teaspoon baking powder
¼ teaspoon salt
¾ cup chopped walnuts
1 cup coconut
½ cup chopped dates

Combine ¼ cup brown sugar and margarine. Work in ½ cup each white and whole-wheat flour until a soft dough forms. Press dough into greased 13 × 9 × 2-inch baking dish. Bake in 350°F oven 15 minutes.

Gradually add ½ cup brown sugar to beaten eggs; continue to beat until light and fluffy. Add vanilla.

Combine dry ingredients, walnuts, coconut, and dates. Spread mixture evenly over baked crust. Return to oven and bake an additional 25 to 30 minutes. Cool, then cut into 24 servings.

southern pecan cake

A delicious change from the traditional frosting.

Yield: 8 servings

2 cups pecan halves
¼ cup butter, melted
¼ cup liquid brown sugar
1 1-layer yellow-cake mix

Arrange pecan halves, top-side-down, in 8-inch-round cake pan.
Combine butter and brown sugar; pour over pecans.
Prepare cake mix as directed. Pour over pecans; bake in a 350°F oven 30 minutes or until done. Cool in pan 5 minutes. Invert pan on serving platter. Wait an additional 5 minutes before removing pan.

english-toffee refrigerator cake

A delicious English version of the American cheesecake.

Yield: 12 servings

2½ ounces unsweetened chocolate
½ cup milk
⅔ cup granulated sugar
5 egg yolks, beaten
1 cup butter
1 cup powdered sugar
5 egg whites
1 cup graham-cracker crumbs
1 cup chopped pecans
1 cup whipped cream

Melt chocolate; cool. Combine milk, granulated sugar, and beaten egg yolks in top of double boiler. Cook over boiling water, stirring constantly, until thickened. Cool.

Cream together butter, powdered sugar, and cooled chocolate. Blend into cooled egg-yolk mixture.

Beat egg whites until stiff. Fold chocolate mixture into egg whites. Blend well.

Combine graham crackers and pecans. Sprinkle ½ the graham-cracker crumb and nut mixture over the bottom of an 8-inch square pan. Pour chocolate mixture into pan; top with remaining crumb and nut mixture. Chill for 24 hours.

To serve, cut cake into squares. Garnish with whipped cream.

brown-sugar and pecan cheesecake

Yield: 12 servings

2 tablespoons butter
1¼ cups zwieback crushed to
resemble crumbs
2 tablespoons brown sugar
¼ cup finely chopped pecans
1 pound cream cheese, softened

½ cup granulated sugar
½ cup brown sugar
3 eggs
2 tablespoons lemon juice
1 cup pecan halves

Melt butter; blend with zwieback, brown sugar, and pecans. Press ¾ of mixture on the bottom of greased 9-inch springform pan. Bake at 350°F for 8 minutes.

Beat cream cheese and sugars until light and fluffy. Beat in eggs and lemon juice; pour over crust. Arrange pecan halves over filling. Sprinkle remaining crust over top of pecans.

Bake for 20 to 25 minutes, until filling is set. Cool before serving. Refrigerate.

butter-pecan torte

Yield: 8 servings

3 egg whites
1 cup granulated sugar
1 teaspoon baking powder
¼ teaspoon cream of tartar
¼ teaspoon salt

1 teaspoon vanilla
1½ cups chopped pecans
1 cup crushed bite-size corn
    breakfast cereal
1 pint butter-pecan ice cream

Beat egg whites until foamy. Add sugar, baking powder, cream of tartar, and salt. Continue to beat until meringue is stiff and dry. Fold in vanilla, 1 cup pecans, and crushed cereal. Spread mixture evenly in a 9-inch buttered pie pan. Bake in preheated 350°F oven 25 minutes or until lightly brown. Cool.

Soften ice cream; spread over cooled torte. Sprinkle top with remaining ½ cup pecans. Freeze to set ice cream.

pistachio cake roll

Yield: 12 servings

5 large eggs
1¾ cups granulated sugar
½ teaspoon salt
2 teaspoons vanilla
1¼ cups all-purpose flour
2 tablespoons cornstarch
3 eggs

1 cup milk
½ cup half-and-half
2 to 3 drops green food coloring
½ cup butter
½ cup chopped pistachio nuts
2 cups whipped cream
½ cup whole pistachio nuts

Beat 5 large eggs until light and fluffy. Gradually add 1 cup sugar, salt, and 1 teaspoon vanilla. Beat until mixture begins to thicken. Fold in flour, a small portion at a time. Pour mixture into a greased and waxed, lined jelly pan. Bake in a 350°F oven 20 minutes or until done.

Remove cake from oven. Turn cake onto a powdered-sugar-dusted cloth. Remove paper and roll in jelly-roll fashion. Wrap ends of towel under cake; allow to cool in the towel.

Combine ¾ cup sugar and cornstarch in top of double boiler.

Beat remaining 3 eggs until fluffy. Add eggs to sugar mixture; beat well to combine. Stir in milk and half-and-half; cook over double boiler until thick. Remove from heat; stir in green food coloring, butter, and 1 teaspoon vanilla. Cool.

Unfold cake; spread with cooled filling. Sprinkle pistachio nuts over cream filling; reroll cake. Chill.

Frost chilled cake roll with whipped cream. Decorate top with whole pistachio nuts. Refrigerate.

walnut spice cake

walnut spice cake

Yield: 12 servings

2 cups all-purpose flour
1⅓ cups granulated sugar
2 teaspoons baking powder
1 teaspoon salt
¼ teaspoon baking soda
1 teaspoon cinnamon
½ teaspoon nutmeg
½ cup butter
½ cup thawed orange-juice
  concentrate
½ cup milk
2 eggs
2 cups whipped cream
1 cup chopped walnuts
12 walnut halves
12 fresh orange sections

Combine flour, sugar, baking powder, salt, soda, and spices. Add butter, orange juice, and milk; beat on low speed for 2 minutes. Add eggs; continue to beat for 2 additional minutes. Pour batter into 2 greased and floured 8-inch cake pans.

Bake cakes at 350°F for 30 to 35 minutes or until done. Remove from pans; cool.

Spread whipped cream between layers; stack layers. Cover tops and sides of cake evenly with whipped cream. Cover sides of cake with chopped walnuts. Decorate top by alternating walnut halves and orange sections around top edge of cake. Refrigerate until ready to serve.

walnut cream layers

Yield: 12 servings

1 prepared 10-inch oblong
    angel-food cake
1 can chocolate pie filling
½ cup whipping cream
¼ cup granulated sugar
1 teaspoon vanilla
1 cup chopped walnuts

Cut angel-food cake into 3 layers. Spread chocolate pie filling between cake layers and on top of cake.

Whip cream until frothy. Gradually add sugar and vanilla; whip until cream stands in soft peaks.

Swirl whipped cream on sides of cake. Sprinkle nuts on sides of cake. Refrigerate to set cake. Cut and serve.

ginger walnut loaf

This is delicious served warm.

Yield: 10 servings

1 15-ounce gingerbread mix
½ cup honey
2 cups coarsely chopped walnuts

Prepare and bake gingerbread mix as directed. Remove from oven; wait 5 minutes before removing from pan.

Remove from pan. Coat top with honey. Spread walnuts over top; press them gently into honey coating.

ginger walnut loaf

fruit cakes and toppings

apple bake cake

apple bake cake

A delicious way to serve apples during the peak of the season.

Yield: 8 servings

2 cups cooked apple slices
¼ cup butter, melted
½ cup liquid brown sugar
¼ cup butter
¾ cup granulated sugar
2 eggs
¼ cup milk
1 cup all-purpose flour
1 teaspoon baking powder
Dash of salt
1 teaspoon vanilla
Confectioners' sugar for top
(optional)

Arrange apples in the bottom of 9-inch-round greased baking dish.

Combine brown sugar and melted butter; pour over apples. Cream ¼ cup butter and granulated sugar until smooth. Add eggs; beat until blended. Add milk alternately with dry ingredients; blend. Stir in vanilla.

Pour dough over apples. Bake cake in 350°F oven 30 minutes or until it tests done. Remove from oven; cool for 5 minutes in the pan before inverting pan onto a cooling rack.

Dust with powdered sugar if desired.

wacky apple cake

The sliced apples and cream form an attractive topping for this cake.

Yield: 1 8-inch cake

2 tablespoons margarine
1 cup granulated sugar
1 egg, beaten
2 cups unbleached flour
2 teaspoons baking powder
1 teaspoon salt
1 teaspoon cinnamon

¾ cup milk
3 or 4 cooking apples, peeled,
 cored, and thinly sliced
2 tablespoons margarine, melted
2 tablespoons granulated sugar
½ cup half-and-half

Cream 2 tablespoons margarine and 1 cup sugar until light and fluffy. Add egg; mix well.

Combine dry ingredients. Add alternately with milk to creamed mixture, mixing well after each addition.

Pour batter into greased 8 × 8-inch cake pan. Cover batter with rows of sliced apples. Pour 2 tablespoons melted margarine over apples; sprinkle with remaining sugar.

Bake in moderate (375°F) oven 30 minutes. Pour half-and-half over cake; return to oven and continue to bake for 30 minutes or until done. Cool before removing from pan.

carolyn's banana cheesecake

Yield: 8 servings

1¼ cups graham-cracker crumbs
¼ cup granulated sugar
⅓ cup margarine, melted
1 8-ounce-package cream cheese,
 softened

1 15-ounce can condensed milk
⅓ cup lemon juice
2 bananas
1 cup whipped cream

In 9-inch pie pan mix crumbs, sugar, and margarine until crumbs are well-moistened. Press mixture evenly on bottom and sides of pan. Bake for 8 minutes at 400°F.

Beat cream cheese until fluffy. Gradually add milk; beat until well-blended. Add lemon juice; blend well.

Mash 1 banana; blend into cream-cheese mixture.

Slice remaining banana over crust. Pour filling on top of bananas. Chill for 4 hours or until firm.

Slice cake into serving sizes; place on dessert plates. Top each serving with a mound of whipped cream.

glazed apricot banana cake

Yield: 1 8-inch loaf cake

1 cup dried apricots
½ cup hot water
1¾ cups unbleached flour
3 teaspoons baking powder
½ teaspoon salt
⅓ cup margarine
⅔ cup granulated sugar
2 eggs, well-beaten
1 cup ripe bananas, mashed

glaze

1 cup powdered sugar
1 teaspoon vanilla
2 tablespoons milk
4 dried apricot halves
4 walnut halves

Cut dried apricots into small pieces; cover with ½ cup hot water. Let soak for 24 hours.

Combine flour, baking powder, and salt; reserve.

Cream margarine and sugar until light and fluffy. Add eggs to cream mixture; mix well. Add dry ingredients and bananas alternately to cream mixture, mixing after each addition only enough to moisten the dry ingredients.

Drain apricots; fold into batter. Pour batter into greased 8 × 4 × 2-inch loaf pan. Bake at 350°F about 1 hour and 10 minutes or until a toothpick inserted in the center comes out clean. Remove cake from pan; cool.

Combine powdered sugar, vanilla, and milk to form a thin glaze. Drizzle glaze over cooled cake.

Garnish with dried apricot and walnut halves.

black-cherry cheesecake

A refreshing summer dessert.

Yield: 1 8-inch cake

1 package cheesecake mix with shell
1 cup sour cream
1 3-ounce package black-cherry gelatin
¾ cup cherry juice and water, boiling
1 cup pitted black cherries
½ cup cold water

Prepare cheesecake mix as directed, mixing 1 cup sour cream with filling before pouring into shell. Chill until firm.

Dissolve gelatin in boiling cherry juice and water. Chill until partially thickened. Stir in black cherries and cold water. Spread over chilled cheesecake. Return cake to refrigerator; chill until firm.

cherry-berry cake

cherry-berry cake

Yield: 8 servings

    ½ cup margarine
    ¾ cup sugar
    1 egg, beaten
    ⅓ cup milk
    2 cups all-purpose flour
    2 teaspoons baking powder
    ½ teaspoon salt
    1 No. 2 can cherry pie filling

Cream margarine and sugar. Add egg; mix well. Blend in milk.
Combine dry ingredients. Add to margarine mixture.
Spread half of batter in greased 8-inch-round container; cover with ¾ can pie filling. Spread with remaining batter; top with remaining filling. Bake cake in 375°F oven 30 minutes or until done.

cherry cheesecake

Yield: 6 servings

2 tablespoons sugar
¼ cup butter, melted
1 package cheesecake mix
   with crust

1 cup cherry pie filling
½ cup frozen sliced
   strawberries

Combine sugar, melted butter, and graham-crackers from cheesecake mix. Press crumb mixture into an 8-inch pie pan, covering bottom and sides. Chill.

Prepare cheesecake filling mix as directed on package; pour into chilled crust. Refrigerate for 2 hours or until filling is set.

Combine pie filling and chilled strawberries. Spoon over chilled filling. Refrigerate for 1 hour to set topping.

lemon cranberry ring

An elegant holiday upside-down cake that forms its own topping as it bakes.

Yield: 1 10-inch cake

1 cup granulated sugar
¼ cup margarine
2¼ cups whole fresh
   cranberries

1 1-pound 2¾-ounce lemon-cake mix
   with pudding
3 eggs
1 cup water
⅓ cup oil

Combine sugar, margarine, and cranberries; mix well. Spread cranberry mixture evenly over bottom of greased and floured 10-inch tube pan.

Mix cake mix, eggs, water, and oil until well-blended.

Turn mixer on high speed; beat for 2 minutes. Pour cake batter over cranberry mixture.

Bake at 350°F for 40 minutes or until done. Remove cake from oven; invert pan on serving plate. Let cake stand 2 minutes before lifting off pan.

rainbow cake

An attractive centerpiece for a backyard barbecue.

Yield: 12 servings

1 recipe Cooked Frosting (see Index)
2 9-inch white-cake layers
1½ cups shredded coconut
1 to 2 drops red food coloring

1 to 2 drops yellow food coloring
1 to 2 drops green food coloring
3 teaspoons milk

Prepare Cooked Frosting; fill and frost tops and sides of cake layers.

Divide coconut evenly among 3 jars. Mix each food coloring with 1 teaspoon milk; pour 1 color in each of the 3 jars of coconut. Cover jars; shake until coconut is evenly tinted. Combine tinted coconut. Cover top and sides of frosted cake.

devil's date delight

The blend of chocolate and dates in this cake will give your taste buds a new sensation.

Yield: 1 2-layer 9-inch cake

1 18.5-ounce devil's-food cake mix
1 cup chopped dates
1 cup hot water
⅛ teaspoon salt
¼ teaspoon lemon rind
2 teaspoons lemon juice
2 tablespoons honey
1 recipe Citrus Frosting (recipe follows)
12 whole dates, pitted
12 walnut halves
¼ cup granulated sugar

Prepare and bake cake mix as directed on package. Remove from oven; cool.
Combine chopped dates and hot water; simmer for 15 minutes. Drain. Add salt, lemon rind, lemon juice, and honey; mix well. Cool mixture. When cool, spread mixture between the devil's-food layers.
Frost cake with Citrus Frosting.
Stuff whole pitted dates with walnut halves; roll them in granulated sugar. Arrange stuffed dates in a circle on top of frosted cake.

citrus frosting

Yield: Approximately 1½ cups

¾ cup granulated sugar
1½ tablespoons flour
¼ teaspoon salt
1 teaspoon grated lemon peel
⅓ cup orange juice
2 tablespoons lemon juice
1 egg, beaten
1 tablespoon butter
1 cup whipping cream

Mix sugar, flour, and salt in top of double boiler. Add grated lemon peel, citrus juices, and egg; mix well. Cook in double boiler until thickened, stirring frequently. Stir in butter; cool.
Whip cream until stiff; fold into cooked mixture.

lime and cinnamon cheesecake

Yield: 6 servings

2 tablespoons sugar
1 teaspoon cinnamon
¼ cup margarine, melted
1 package cheesecake mix with crust
1½ cups cold milk

2 tablespoons lime juice
2 to 3 drops green food coloring
1 can pressurized whipped topping
6 thin lime slices

Dissolve sugar and cinnamon in melted margarine. Stir in graham crackers from mix until well-moistened. Press crumb mixture into 8-inch pie pan, covering bottom and sides. Chill.

Pour milk into mixing bowl. Add filling mixture; blend about 1 minute. Add lime juice and food coloring; continue to beat for an additional 3 minutes or until mixture thickens. Pour into chilled pie shell. Refrigerate for 2 hours before serving.

To serve, slice and place on serving dishes. Top with a mound of whipped topping. Cut lime slices in half and twist on top of whipped-cream mound.

creole chocolate cake

A cake for the chocolate-covered-raisin-lover in your family.

Yield: 1 2-layer 9-inch cake

1 2-layer chocolate-cake mix
1 teaspoon cinnamon
½ teaspoon nutmeg
½ teaspoon allspice

½ cup chopped raisins
½ cup chopped walnuts
1 can prepared chocolate frosting

To the cake-mix powder add cinnamon, nutmeg, and allspice. Prepare and bake cake mix as directed in 2 9-inch-round cake pans. Cool.

Stir chopped raisins and nuts into prepared frosting. Frost layers, covering tops and sides.

strawberry chocolate layers

Yield: 1 2-layer 9-inch cake

2 9-inch chocolate-cake layers
3 cups whipped cream

1 cup crushed strawberries
1 cup whole fresh strawberries

Using a sharp knife or a thread, split cake layers in half horizontally.

Combine 2½ cups whipped cream with crushed strawberries; spread evenly between the cake layers.

Spread remaining ½ cup whipped cream over top of cake. Arrange whole strawberries in rings on top of whipped cream.

double-orange surprise layers

Yield: 12 servings

    ¾ cup orange marmalade
    2 9-inch yellow-cake layers

orange glaze

    2 cups powdered sugar
    2 tablespoons cornstarch
    ¼ cup orange juice
    1 cup toasted almonds

Spread marmalade between cake layers; place on serving platter.

Combine powdered sugar and cornstarch. Beat in orange juice until a smooth glaze forms.

Drizzle glaze over top of cake. Sprinkle with toasted almonds.

orange cheesecake

Have all ingredients at room temperature.

Yield: 16 servings

    ½ cup margarine
    ¾ cup granulated sugar
    3 tablespoons milk
    1 cup all-purpose flour
    4 eggs
    ½ teaspoon baking powder
    1 teaspoon grated orange rind
    2 8-ounce packages cream cheese
    1 tablespoon flour
    3 tablespoons thawed frozen
        orange-juice concentrate
    1½ cups milk
    Fresh orange slices for garnish

Combine margarine, ¼ cup granulated sugar, 3 tablespoons milk, 1 cup flour, 1 egg, baking powder, and orange rind. Mix until well-blended. Spread mixture in a well-greased 10-inch springform pan.

Cream remaining sugar and cream cheese until fluffy. Add 3 eggs; beat in. Stir in 1 tablespoon flour, orange-juice concentrate, and 1½ cups milk. Beat until smooth. Pour batter over dough.

Bake for 1 hour at 300°F. Remove from oven; cool completely before removing sides of pan. Garnish with fresh orange slices.

orange cheesecake

gingerbread orange ring

A quick yet fancy dessert for a late-night supper.

Yield: 8 servings

1 15-ounce gingerbread mix
½ cup whipping cream
2 tablespoons granulated sugar

1 teaspoon vanilla
1 teaspoon dried orange rind
½ cup mandarin oranges

Prepare gingerbread mix as directed. Bake cake in 1-quart greased and floured ring mold in 350°F oven 40 minutes or until done.

Whip cream until peaks form. Fold in granulated sugar, vanilla, and orange rind.

Invert gingerbread on serving platter; wait 5 minutes before removing pan.

To serve, mound whipped cream in the center of cooled gingerbread ring. Top with mandarin orange slices.

harvest cake

A traditional dessert served in the harvest fields of Kansas.

Yield: 16 servings

- 1¾ cups sugar
- ⅔ cup margarine
- 3 eggs
- 1 teaspoon vanilla
- 2½ cups all-purpose flour
- 1½ teaspoons baking soda
- ½ teaspoon salt
- 1 cup buttermilk
- 2 packets liquid chocolate
- ½ cup boiling water
- 1 quart peaches with juice, sliced

Cream sugar and margarine until light and fluffy. Add eggs individually, beating well after each addition. Mix in vanilla.

Sift together dry ingredients; add to sugar mixture alternately with buttermilk. Dissolve chocolate in boiling water and mix into batter. Pour into a greased and floured 13 × 9-inch oblong pan. Bake at 350°F for 40 minutes or until done. Cool.

To serve, slice cake and place in serving dishes. Cover each piece with ¼ cup sliced peaches with juice. Serve immediately.

pineapple spice layer

A delicious combination of fruit and spices.

Yield: 1 8-inch layer cake

- ¼ cup butter
- ¼ cup liquid brown sugar
- 4 pineapple slices, drained
- 1 8-ounce spice-cake mix
  (1-layer size)

Melt butter in an 8-inch layer-cake pan; stir in brown sugar. Arrange pineapple slices in bottom of pan containing butter and sugar mixture.

Prepare cake mix as directed. Pour cake batter over pineapple and butter mixture. Bake in 350°F oven 30 minutes or until a toothpick inserted in center comes out clean. Invert pan on serving platter; let rest 5 minutes before removing pan. Serve cake warm.

pineapple crown

The blend of spices and pineapple give this dessert a delightful flavor.

Yield: 8 servings

1 1-layer spice-cake mix
1 recipe Cream-Cheese Frosting (see
**   Index)**
3 egg yolks, beaten
2 tablespoons cornstarch
1 8-ounce can crushed pineapple in
**   heavy syrup**
1 cup sugar
2 tablespoons butter
2 tablespoons lemon juice

Prepare and bake cake mix as directed. Remove from pan; cool.

Prepare frosting. Frost sides of cooled cake and a 1-inch ring around the outer edge of the cake top.

Combine remaining ingredients in a heavy saucepan; cook over low heat until thick. Cool. Spread over top of frosted cake within the perimeters of the icing.

pineapple stacks

Yield: 1 2-layer 9-inch cake

⅔ cup drained pineapple syrup
⅓ cup butter, melted
⅓ cup liquid brown sugar
1 1-pound 4-ounce can crushed
**   pineapple, drained**
1 18.5-ounce white-cake mix

Combine pineapple syrup, melted butter, and brown sugar. Divide this mixture into 2 9-inch-round layer pans. Cover with drained pineapple.

Prepare cake mix as directed. Divide dough evenly between the fruit-filled cake pans. Bake for 30 minutes in 350°F oven or until a toothpick inserted in center comes out clean. Invert pans; wait 5 minutes to remove pans.

To serve, place one layer on top of the other before slicing.

raisin cherry loaf

The fruit adds the decorative touch when this cake is sliced.

Yield: 12 servings

1 cup raisins
½ cup whole candied cherries
½ cup rum
1½ cups all-purpose flour
3 teaspoons baking powder
½ teaspoon salt

¾ cup granulated sugar
¾ cup shortening
2 eggs, beaten
1 teaspoon vanilla
1 recipe Milk Glaze I (see Index)

Combine raisins, cherries, and rum; heat to boiling. Remove from heat; let stand overnight to absorb rum.

Combine flour, baking powder, salt, and sugar. Cut in shortening until mixture resembles a fine cornmeal. Add eggs and vanilla; mix well. Stir in fruit with rum. Spread batter into greased 9-inch loaf pan.

Bake cake at 350°F for 1 hour or until done. Remove from pan. Top with Milk Glaze.

raisin cherry loaf

cheesecake torte

Yield: 8 servings

1 9-inch yellow-cake layer
½ cup strawberry jam
1 8-ounce package cream cheese,
    softened
1 15-ounce can condensed milk
⅓ cup lemon juice
1 cup strawberry pie filling
1 cup whipped topping

Cut a piece of waxed paper 2 inches high and long enough to wrap tightly around the cake layer. Cut a piece of cardboard the same size; wrap it tightly around the waxed paper. Fasten with tape.

Spread top of cake layer with strawberry jam.

Beat cream cheese until fluffy. Gradually add milk; beat until well-blended. Add lemon juice; blend. Chill 1 cup of this filling until semi-set. Spread over jam; return to refrigerator until set. (Make tarts from remaining filling.)

Slice cake into serving pieces; place on dessert plates. Top each serving with 2 tablespoons pie filling. Using a pastry bag and rosette tube, decorate each slice with a whipped-cream rosette.

springtime cheesecake

A delightful way to combine the plentiful fruits of spring. Use your favorite cheesecake recipe, or try one of the recipes in this book.

Yield: 10 servings

1 9-inch prepared cheesecake
    without topping
1 small banana, sliced
1 tablespoon lemon juice
½ cup canned peach slices, drained
½ cup canned pineapple chunks,
    drained
½ cup fresh strawberry halves
¼ cup Thompson seedless grapes
¼ cup English-walnut halves
1 cup canned fruit juice
1½ teaspoons cornstarch

Prepare cheesecake; let set until firm.

Slice banana; coat with lemon juice to prevent browning. Arrange fruits and nuts on top of cheesecake. Refrigerate.

Combine fruit juice and cornstarch; stir until smooth. Heat mixture until thickened. Cool glaze to lukewarm; pour over fruit. Return to refrigerator; chill thoroughly.

crown jewels

A dessert fit for the royal family.

Yield: 12 servings

1 cup all-purpose white flour
1 cup whole-wheat flour
2 teaspoons baking powder
1½ teaspoons baking soda
½ teaspoon salt
2 teaspoons apple-pie spice
1 cup granulated sugar
1 cup brown sugar
1½ cups oil

4 eggs, beaten
2 cups grated carrots
1 8½-ounce can crushed pineapple, drained
½ cup chopped almonds
2 cups powdered sugar, sifted
2 to 3 tablespoons hot milk
½ cup candied fruit
½ cup slivered almonds

Combine flours, baking powder, soda, salt, and apple-pie spice. Add sugars, oil, and eggs; mix with electric beater for 2 minutes. Add carrots, pineapple, and nuts; stir in. Pour into 2 greased and floured 9-inch cake pans. Bake at 350°F for 35 to 40 minutes or until done. Cool; remove from pans.

Combine powdered sugar and enough hot milk to form a pourable icing; mix until smooth. Spread a small amount of icing between layers; stack layers. Drizzle remaining icing over top and sides of cake.

Combine fruit and almonds. Sprinkle over top of cake, as shown.

crown jewels

chocolate bundt-lettes*

chocolate bundt *-lettes

Yield: 6 servings

1 1-layer devil's-food cake mix
½ cup corn syrup
¼ cup hot water
¼ cup butter
1 12-ounce package chocolate chips
½ cup chopped pistachios

Prepare cake mix as directed.

Grease and flour Bundt*-Lette pans; fill with batter. Bake at 350°F for 35 to 40 minutes or until done. Cool; remove from pans.

Combine corn syrup, hot water, and butter in saucepan; bring to a boil. Remove from heat; stir in chocolate chips until mixture is well-blended. Cool to warm; spoon over cakes. Sprinkle frosted cakes with pistachios. Let frosting set before serving.

*Registered U.S. Pat. Office (Nordic Ware)

triple-chocolate stacks

A treat for a true chocolate lover.

Yield: 2 dozen cupcakes

1¾ cups sugar
⅔ cup margarine, softened
3 eggs
1 teaspoon vanilla
2½ cups all-purpose flour
1½ teaspoons baking soda
¼ teaspoon salt
1 cup sour milk
2 packets liquid chocolate
½ cup boiling water
1 can prepared chocolate frosting
½ cup chocolate sprinkles

Cream sugar and margarine until light and fluffy. Add eggs individually, beating well after each addition. Mix in vanilla.

Sift together dry ingredients; add to creamed mixture alternately with sour milk.

Dissolve chocolate in boiling water; add to batter. Mix well.

Fill cupcake papers ⅔ full of batter. Bake at 350°F for 25 minutes or until done. Cool.

Prepare frosting; frost top of cooled cupcakes. Sprinkle chocolate sprinkles over frosted tops.

chocolate tea cakes

Yield: 32 cakes

1 10-inch-square yellow-cake layer

chocolate glaze

½ cup light corn syrup
⅓ cup hot water
4 tablespoons margarine
1 12-ounce package chocolate chips

Cut cake into 2-inch strips. Cut each strip into 4 equal pieces. Cut each piece into 2 triangles.

Combine corn syrup, water, and margarine in saucepan; bring to a boil. Continue to heat until butter melts. Remove from heat. Stir in chocolate chips until they melt. Cool to room temperature.

Place each cake triangle onto a 2-prong frying fork. Spoon cooled Chocolate Glaze over cakes until well-covered. Place on cooling rack to allow excess chocolate to drip from cakes.

chocolate tea cakes

chocolate igloo

An ideal way to use leftover cake.

Yield: 8 to 10 servings

1 9-inch-square chocolate cake
2 quarts pineapple sherbet
1 cup whipped cream
Maraschino cherry

Slice cake layer into 2 parts, using a sharp knife or a string. Cut cake layers into triangular wedges.

Coat 2-quart bowl with butter; press cake triangles against sides to form a design, as illustrated.

Soften pineapple sherbet; mold in 2-quart bowl against cake lining. Cover top with cake triangles. Freeze until firm.

To serve, unmold onto serving platter and garnish with whipped cream and cherry.

chocolate igloo

46

hot-fudge sundaes

This recipe gives a different twist to the traditional hot-fudge sundae.

Yield: 8 servings

6 egg whites
⅓ cup sugar
1 quart French-vanilla ice cream

8 shortcake shells
1 cup hot-fudge sauce
¼ cup chopped salted mixed nuts

Beat egg whites until stiff. Add sugar gradually; continue to beat until meringue stands in peaks.

Place ½ cup ice cream into center of each shell. Cover ice cream and shell completely with meringue. Bake in 450°F oven about 4 minutes or until meringue starts to turn light brown.

Heat hot-fudge sauce until warm.

Place dessert in serving dishes. Spoon hot-fudge sauce over baked meringue. Sprinkle with chopped nuts. Serve immediately.

goober cakes

Yield: 24 cupcakes

1 2-layer chocolate-cake mix
1 recipe Peanut-Butter Cream-Cheese
    Frosting (recipe follows)
1 cup chopped salted peanuts

Prepare cake mix as directed. Fill cupcake papers ⅔ full of batter. Bake as directed on package. Cool.

Mix frosting; frost tops of cooled cupcakes. Sprinkle chopped peanuts over frosted cupcakes.

peanut-butter cream-cheese frosting

Yield: 1¾ cups

6 ounces cream cheese, softened
¼ cup smooth peanut butter
1 teaspoon vanilla
3 cups powdered sugar

Beat cream cheese, peanut butter, and vanilla together until smooth. Gradually add sugar. Beat until fluffy.

blueberry mounds

A quick dessert for unexpected company.

Yield: 8 servings

8 prepared Mary Ann shells
1 can blueberry pie filling
1 can pressurized whipped topping

Place Mary Ann shells in serving dishes. Pour ⅓ cup pie filling in center of each Mary Ann shell. Top with whipped topping flower made with tip of pressurized can. Refrigerate.

butterscotch fondue

An excellent way to use pieces of leftover cake.

Yield: 4 servings

butterscotch sauce

1 6-ounce package butterscotch
   chips
⅓ cup whipping cream
1 tablespoon white corn syrup

2 cups 1-inch cake cubes
½ cup chopped pecans
½ cup shredded coconut

Melt butterscotch chips over boiling water. Stir in cream and corn syrup, beating constantly. Continue to beat until a smooth mixture develops. Pour into fondue dish.

To serve, dip cake cubes into Butterscotch Sauce, then into nuts or coconut.

chocolate fondue

Yield: 4 servings

1 can chocolate syrup
¼ cup brandy
2 cups cake cubes

½ cup chopped pecans
½ cup chopped raisins
½ cup chopped coconut

Heat chocolate syrup to warm. Stir in brandy. Pour into fondue dish.

To serve, dip cake squares into chocolate sauce, then into choice of toppings.

mushroom caps

The pan used to bake a decorative cake need not be expensive. The cakes shown here were baked in 4-ounce mushroom cans. Just remember that, for baking, the container must be ovenproof and free from ridges. Fill approximately ⅔ full of batter and, if small, bake as for cupcakes, or, if container is approximately equal to a cake pan, bake as a cake layer.

Yield: 6 to 8 servings

1 1-layer devils-food cake mix

chocolate glaze

¼ cup light corn syrup
2 tablespoons hot water
2 tablespoons butter
1 6-ounce package chocolate chips

Prepare cake mix as directed. Fill greased and floured small cans ⅔ full; bake as instructed for cupcakes. Cool 5 minutes in cans; remove from cans to cool.

Combine corn syrup, water, and butter in a saucepan; bring to a boil. Continue to heat until butter melts. Remove from heat. Stir in chocolate chips until they melt. Cool to room temperature.

Place cakes on a rack that is resting on waxed paper. Spoon Chocolate Glaze over cakes until covered. Let glaze set before serving.

mushroom caps

fruitcake petits fours

An interesting way to use leftover Christmas fruitcake.

Yield: 30 servings

1 small loaf fruitcake
1 6-ounce package chocolate chips
2 tablespoons butter, melted

Slice fruitcake into triangular-shape wedges, or cut designs from cake, using small cookie cutters.

Melt chocolate chips over boiling water. Add melted butter; stir until smooth. Drizzle chocolate over small cakes. Allow chocolate to set before serving.

quick petits fours

Yield: 32 servings

1 8-inch loaf angel-food cake

chocolate topping

1 pint whipped topping
2 tablespoons granulated sugar

1 tablespoon cocoa
1 cup angel-flake coconut

Cut cake into 2-inch squares.
Blend whipped topping, sugar, and cocoa.
Roll cake squares in Chocolate Topping; sprinkle with coconut.

united nations cupcakes

A novel way to study geography.

Yield: 10 cupcakes

1 1-layer spice-cake mix
1 recipe Mae's Seven-Minute
**   Frosting (see Index)**
10 miniature flags from
**   various nations**

Prepare and bake cupcakes as directed on package. Cool.
Prepare frosting recipe. Frost cupcakes by holding each cupcake by the bottom and swirling the top in the frosting. Place a flag in the center of each cupcake.

pound cake a la mode

Yield: 8 servings

1 purchased pound cake
1 quart French-vanilla ice cream
1 cup Sherry Butter Sauce
    (recipe follows)
8 mint leaves

Slice pound cake into 8 slices. Place on serving dishes. Top each slice with a scoop of ice cream. Spoon 2 tablespoons Sherry Butter Sauce over ice cream. Top with a mint leaf.

sherry butter sauce

Yield: Approximately 1 cup

¼ cup margarine, melted
1 cup sugar
1 tablespoon water
2 tablespoons lemon juice
¼ cup sherry wine

Combine margarine, sugar, and water in saucepan; cook until thick. Stir in lemon juice and wine. Cool to lukewarm.

pound-cake pudding

A quick and easy dessert for a late-night supper.

Yield: 6 servings

1 package regular butterscotch
    pudding
1 8-inch loaf pound cake
1 can pressurized whipped topping

Prepare butterscotch pudding according to directions on package.
Cut pound cake in half lengthwise. With a 2-inch cookie cutter, cut each lengthwise strip into 3 circles. Arrange cake circles in dessert dishes. Pour butterscotch pudding over each circle. Garnish with whipped topping.

coffee cakes

banana fruitcake

This cake offers a change from the heavy traditional fruitcake.

Yield: 1 9-inch loaf cake

1 16-ounce pound-cake mix
½ cup water
½ cup mashed bananas
2 eggs, beaten
1 cup chopped candied mixed fruit
½ cup chopped almonds
2 ounces cream cheese, softened
½ cup butter
1 teaspoon vanilla
½ box powdered sugar
1 cup slivered almonds
3 red candied cherries
3 green candied cherries

banana fruitcake

Reserve 2 tablespoons cake-mix powder for later use. Combine remaining cake mix, water, bananas, and eggs; mix until cake mix is moistened. Set mixer on medium speed; beat batter 3 minutes.

Combine candied fruit, almonds, and reserved cake mix; mix thoroughly; fold into cake batter.

Pour batter into greased and floured 9-inch loaf pan. Bake in 325°F oven for 60 to 65 minutes or until done. Remove from pan to cool.

While cake is cooling, combine cream cheese, butter, vanilla, and powdered sugar. Beat until smooth.

Spread cooled loaf with frosting. Decorate with almonds and cherries, as shown.

baked blackberry pudding cake

Yield: 8 servings

⅓ cup butter
⅔ cup sugar
1 egg, beaten
½ cup milk
1 teaspoon vanilla
¼ teaspoon salt
1½ cups flour
2 teaspoons baking powder
½ cup canned blackberries,
    drained
1 recipe Blackberry Sauce (recipe
    follows)

Cream butter and sugar until fluffy. Add egg; mix well.

Combine milk and vanilla; add alternately with combined dry ingredients to creamed mixture, beating well after each addition.

Pour batter into greased and floured 8-inch cake pan. Top with blackberries. Bake for 25 to 30 minutes in 350°F oven.

Cut into squares while warm. Serve with Blackberry Sauce.

blackberry sauce

Yield: Approximately 1 cup

⅔ cup granulated sugar
2 tablespoons flour
¼ teaspoon salt
1 cup black-cherry juice and water
2 tablespoons butter
2 tablespoons lemon juice
⅔ cup blackberries

Blend sugar, flour, and salt. Stir in 1 cup liquid. Add remaining ingredients. Cook, stirring constantly, until mixture thickens.

Serve sauce warm over Baked Blackberry Pudding Cake.

cherry braid

Yield: 1 braid

1 cake compressed yeast
1 cup warm water
¼ cup sugar
¼ cup shortening, melted
1 teaspoon salt
1 egg, beaten

4 to 5 cups all-purpose white flour
¾ cup wild-cherry preserves
1 recipe Cream-Cheese Frosting
  (see Index)
2 to 3 drops red food coloring
6 pecan halves

Dissolve yeast in warm water. Add sugar, shortening, salt, and egg; mix. Work flour into batter until a soft dough forms. Pour dough onto floured surface. Knead for 10 minutes or until folds form in dough. (Add more flour to dough if needed to prevent sticking.) Place in greased bowl. Grease top. Cover dough. Let rise until double in bulk.

Punch down dough. Let rest 10 minutes.

Divide dough into 3 pieces. Roll each piece into a 5 × 15-inch rectangle. Spread ¼ cup preserves down middle of each rectangle. Roll as for jelly roll; seal firmly. Lay each roll 1 inch apart on greased cookie sheet. Braid by starting in center and working toward each end. Let rise until almost doubled.

Bake braid in 375°F oven 30 minutes or until done.

While braid is baking, mix Cream-Cheese Frosting. Add red food coloring to frosting until a light red. Spread frosting over braid while still warm. Decorate top with pecan halves. Serve braid warm.

peach surprise layer

A different cake to serve for Sunday brunch.

Yield: 8 servings

6 canned peach halves,
  well-drained
¾ cup sugar
¼ cup butter
2 eggs
½ cup milk

1 cup all-purpose flour
1 teaspoon baking powder
Dash of salt
1 teaspoon vanilla
½ cup powdered sugar

Place peaches cut-side-down in well-greased 9-inch-square pan.

Cream sugar and butter until smooth. Add eggs; beat until blended. Add milk alternately with combined flour, baking powder, and salt; blend. Stir in vanilla.

Pour dough over peaches. Bake in 350°F oven 30 minutes or until done. Remove from oven; dust with powdered sugar. Slice; serve cake warm.

date cake

The latticework and crumb topping provide an interesting decoration for this cake.

Yield: 2 cakes

1 cup chopped and pitted dates
2 tablespoons liquid brown sugar
⅔ cup hot water
½ cup chopped walnuts
1 tablespoon fresh lemon juice
1 teaspoon grated lemon rind
1 package active dry yeast
1 cup warm milk
1 teaspoon salt
¼ cup butter, melted
½ cup honey
2 eggs, beaten
5 to 5½ cups unbleached white
      flour
1 egg yolk
2 tablespoons milk
2 tablespoons butter
2 tablespoons granulated sugar
⅓ cup unbleached white flour
½ teaspoon cinnamon

Combine dates, brown sugar, ⅔ cup hot water, nuts, lemon juice, and lemon rind in saucepan. Bring to boil over medium heat, stirring constantly. Continue boiling until mixture is thick enough to spread. Cool.

Dissolve yeast in 1 cup warm milk. Add salt, ¼ cup butter, honey, and 2 beaten eggs; mix well. Work in enough flour to make a stiff dough. Knead for 10 minutes or until folds form in dough. Place in greased bowl. Grease top. Cover dough. Let rise until double in bulk.

Punch down dough. Knead for 2 minutes. Divide dough in half. Roll out each half into an oblong about 16 × 8-inches. Spread half the date filling down center third of each oblong. Cut slits in the dough along each side of the filling, making strips about 1 inch wide. Fold strips at an angle across filling, alternating from side to side. Place on greased baking sheet. Cover. Let rise until double in bulk.

Brush braid with mixture of 1 egg yolk and 2 tablespoons milk.

Combine 2 tablespoons butter, sugar, ⅓ cup flour, and cinnamon until a crumb consistency develops. Sprinkle mixture on top of braids. Bake in preheated 350°F oven 30 minutes or until done.

jule kaga

Yield: 1 loaf

1 package active dry yeast
1 cup warm water
½ cup margarine, melted
½ cup granulated sugar
1 teaspoon salt
4 to 4½ cups unbleached
  white flour
1½ teaspoons ground cardamom
½ cup raisins
½ cup chopped candied fruit
¼ cup chopped blanched almonds
1 recipe Milk Glaze I (recipe
  follows)
¼ cup candied cherry halves
½ cup blanched whole almonds
6 citron slivers

Dissolve yeast in warm water. Add margarine, sugar, and salt; mix well. Work in enough flour to develop a stiff dough. Knead for 10 minutes or until dough is elastic. Place in greased bowl. Grease top of loaf. Cover. Let rise until doubled in bulk.

Punch down dough. Knead in cardamom, raisins, candied fruit, and almonds. Form dough into a round ball; place on large greased baking sheet. Cover. Let rise until doubled in bulk.

Bake dough ball in 400°F oven 10 minutes. Reduce heat to 350°F; continue baking 40 minutes or until loaf is golden brown. Cool.

Frost cooled loaf with Milk Glaze. Decorate loaf by forming flowers, using the cherry halves as centers, surrounded by petals made from whole almonds, and stems made from citron slivers.

milk glaze I

Yield: ½ cup

1 cup powdered sugar
1½ tablespoons milk
¼ teaspoon vanilla

Combine ingredients; beat until creamy.

hazelnut coffee cake

This bread can be used in a low-cholesterol diet.

Yield: 12 servings

¾ cup brown sugar
1 cup all-purpose white flour
1 cup whole-wheat flour
1 teaspoon baking soda
1 teaspoon baking powder
1 teaspoon cinnamon
1 teaspoon nutmeg
½ teaspoon salt

⅔ cup skim milk
1½ ounces liquid egg substitute
¼ cup honey
½ cup ground hazelnuts
1 cup powdered sugar, sifted
1 to 2 tablespoons hot milk
½ cup whole hazelnuts

Mix brown sugar, flours, soda, baking powder, cinnamon, nutmeg, and salt.

Combine milk, egg substitute, and honey. Add liquid mixture to dry ingredients; blend well. Fold in ground hazelnuts. Pour mixture into greased 9-inch loaf pan. Bake at 350°F for 60 minutes or until done. Cool slightly; remove from pan.

Combine powdered sugar and hot milk; beat until smooth. Drizzle over top of cake in a lattice design, as illustrated. Place whole hazelnuts between lattice design.

dutch plum cake

Yield: 8 servings

¾ cup granulated sugar
¼ cup shortening
2 eggs
¼ cup milk
½ cup all-purpose flour
½ cup whole-wheat flour
1 teaspoon baking powder

Dash of salt
1 teaspoon vanilla
1½ cups fresh purple
  plum halves
½ cup chopped pecans
¼ cup brown sugar
½ teaspoon cinnamon

Cream granulated sugar and shortening until smooth. Add eggs; beat until blended. Add milk alternately with combined flours, baking powder, and salt; blend. Stir in vanilla. Pour dough into greased and floured 9-inch-square cake pan. Top dough with plum halves.

Combine pecans, brown sugar, and cinnamon. Sprinkle over plum halves. Bake in 350°F oven 30 minutes or until done.

hazelnut coffee cake

lemon-nut round

By selectively cutting the top of this cake, a decorative touch is created.

Yield: 1 cake

1 package active dry yeast
1½ cups warm water
1½ cups granulated sugar
2 eggs, beaten
1½ cups butter, melted
1 teaspoon salt
2 teaspoons grated lemon peel

5 to 6 cups all-purpose white flour
2 teaspoons cinnamon
¾ cup raisins
1 cup chopped English walnuts
1 recipe Lemon Glaze (recipe
  follows)

Dissolve yeast in warm water. Add ½ cup sugar, the eggs, ½ cup butter, salt, and lemon peel; mix well. Add 3 cups flour; mix in.

Pour 1 cup flour on kneading surface. Pour batter mixture on top of flour; cover with 1 cup flour. Knead until flour is worked into dough. Continue adding flour until a stiff dough has formed. Knead dough 10 minutes or until folds form in it. Place dough in greased bowl. Grease top of dough. Cover. Let rise until double in bulk.

Punch down dough. Knead for 2 minutes. Roll dough into 16 × 12-inch rectangle. Spread ½ cup butter on top of ¾ of dough. (Leave a 16 × 3-inch piece of dough plain).

Combine 1 cup sugar, cinnamon, raisins, and nuts. Spread this evenly over buttered dough. Roll dough as for a jelly roll, up to ¼ plain piece of dough. At this point fold the plain dough under the roll. Place roll in greased tube pan. Seal edge with a knife. Slit top of roll completely around the circle. Pour ½ cup butter over roll. Cover roll; let rise until doubled in bulk.

Bake roll in 350°F oven 45 minutes or until golden brown. Remove from pan; cover with Lemon Glaze. Serve cake warm.

lemon glaze

Yield: ¾ cup

2 cups powdered sugar
1 tablespoon cornstarch
3 tablespoons milk
2 tablespoons lemon juice
1 teaspoon vanilla

Combine dry ingredients. Slowly add liquids, beating constantly. Continue to beat until smooth.

lemon-nut round

lattice raisin coffee cake

The dough gives an interesting design to this cake.

Yield: 24 servings

   1 package active dry yeast
   1 cup warm water
   ¼ cup honey
   ¼ cup butter, melted
   1 teaspoon salt
   1 egg, beaten
   2½ cups whole-wheat flour
   2 to 2½ cups all-purpose white
      flour
   2 cups raisin pie filling
   2 tablespoons butter, melted

Dissolve yeast in warm water. Add honey, butter, salt, and egg; mix well. Work flours into batter until a soft dough forms. Pour dough onto floured surface. Knead for 10 minutes or until folds form in the dough. (Add more flour to dough if needed to prevent sticking.) Place in greased bowl. Grease top. Cover dough; let rise until doubled in bulk.

Punch down dough; let rest 10 minutes. Reserve ¼ of dough; roll remainder of dough to fit a jelly-roll pan. Grease pan; fit dough to bottom of pan. Spread pie filling on top of dough. Roll reserved dough to ¼ inch thick; cut into lattice strips. Crisscross lattice strips over top of raisin filling. Seal edges. Let rise until almost doubled in bulk.

Bake cake at 350°F for 30 minutes or until done. Brush warm latticework with butter. Serve coffee cake warm.

poppy–nut cake

snowcapped coffee cake

Yield: 12 servings

¼ cup shortening
1 cup sugar
2 egg yolks, beaten
1 cup all-purpose white flour
½ cup whole-wheat flour
2 teaspoons baking powder
½ teaspoon salt
½ cup milk
1 teaspoon vanilla
2 egg whites, beaten stiff
½ cup brown sugar
1½ teaspoons cinnamon
1 cup chopped pecans
½ cup chopped raisins
2 tablespoons flour
2 tablespoons butter, melted
2 cups marshmallow cream

Cream shortening and sugar until light and fluffy. Add beaten egg yolks; mix well.

Combine flours, baking powder, and salt. Add dry ingredients alternately with milk and vanilla to creamed mixture; mix well. Fold in beaten egg whites. Place ½ mixture in greased and floured 9 × 2-inch round cake pan.

Combine brown sugar, cinnamon, pecans, raisins, 2 tablespoons flour, and melted butter; mix thoroughly. Spread over batter in cake pan; top with remaining dough. Bake in 350°F oven 30 minutes or until done. Cool; remove from pan.

Soften marshmallow cream; spoon over cake.

snowcapped coffee cake

sugar and candy toppings

ornamental icings

To enable the cake decorations to hold their shape, the icing used for decorating needs to be of a stiffer consistency than that used for the frosting.

Following are two basic recipes for you to use in cake decorating. If you have a favorite recipe, you can use these recipes as guidelines to adapt your recipes for use in cake decorating.

butter cream frosting

Yield: Approximately 3 cups

1 cup butter, softened
5 cups powdered sugar, sifted
1 egg, beaten
1-2 tablespoons water

Cream butter until light and fluffy. Add 2½ cups sifted powdered sugar; beat vigorously until smooth. Add beaten egg; mix well. Beat in remaining powdered sugar. Pour in water, beating until frosting becomes fluffy.

basic royal icing

Yield: Approximately 3 cups

7 cups powdered sugar, sifted
2 tablespoons lemon juice
3 egg whites

Combine the sugar, lemon juice and 1 unbeaten egg white in a large bowl. Stir with a wooden spoon until the mixture is of spreading consistency, adding remaining unbeaten egg white, a small amount at a time, as needed, to get the consistency you desire.

Note: To color icings, add a small amount of color paste. Mix weil before adding more color paste to obtain desired shades.

angel fingers

Yield: 2½ dozen servings

1 9-inch angel-food cake loaf
2 6-ounce packages butterscotch
chips
2 tablespoons white corn syrup
1 cup chopped walnuts

Cut cake into 3 x 4 x 2-inch strips.

Melt butterscotch chips in shallow pan. Stir in corn syrup. Cool slightly.

Using tongs, coat cake pieces with butterscotch, making sure all sides are covered. Remove cake strips from butterscotch; coat with nuts. Place on waxed paper to set butterscotch.

almond raisin cake

An old-world favorite recipe.

Yield: 12 servings

½ cup milk
½ cup granulated sugar
½ teaspoon salt
¼ cup butter
¼ cup warm water
1 package active dry yeast
2 eggs, beaten
2½ cups all-purpose flour
½ cup raisins
½ teaspoon grated citron
½ cup chopped almonds
½ cup powdered sugar, sifted

Scald milk. Stir in granulated sugar, salt, and butter. Cool to lukewarm.

Measure warm water into large bowl; sprinkle in yeast. Stir until dissolved. Stir in lukewarm-milk mixture. Beat in eggs and flour; beat about 5 minutes. Cover; let rise until doubled in bulk.

Grease and flour a 1½-quart tube mold.

Stir down batter; beat vigorously for 3 minutes. Stir in raisins, citron, and almonds. Pour batter into prepared mold; let rise until doubled in bulk.

Bake cake in 350°F oven 1 hour or until done. Let rest in pan 5 minutes before removing. Dust warm cake with powdered sugar.

picture on following pages: almond rasin cake

almond raisin nut cake

All this delicious nut bread needs is a simple powdered-sugar dusting for a decorative touch.

Yield: 12 servings

2 cups all-purpose flour
¾ cup granulated sugar
½ cup brown sugar
1½ teaspoons baking soda
1½ teaspoons salt
1 teaspoon cinnamon
½ teaspoon nutmeg
½ cup margarine

1½ cups applesauce
2 eggs
½ cup chopped figs
¾ cup raisins
¼ cup citron
¾ cup blanched whole almonds
½ cup powdered sugar, sifted

Combine flour, granulated and brown sugars, soda, salt, cinnamon, and nutmeg in mixing bowl. Add margarine and applesauce; beat on low speed of electric mixer 2 minutes, being sure to scrape sides of bowl. Add eggs; beat another 2 minutes. Stir in fruits and nuts.

Pour batter into greased and floured 9-inch loaf pan. Bake cake at 350°F for 1½ hours or until done. Cool slightly before removing from pan. Dust warm cake with sifted powdered sugar. Serve cake warm.

almond-brickle layer

Yield: 16 servings

½ cup margarine
½ cup liquid brown sugar
½ cup granulated sugar
2 cups unbleached white flour
1 teaspoon baking powder

1 egg, beaten
1 cup buttermilk
1 teaspoon vanilla
¾ cup crushed almond brickle
½ cup chopped almonds

Combine margarine, sugars, and flour; beat until well-blended. Reserve ½ cup for topping. Add baking powder, egg, buttermilk, and vanilla to remaining mixture; blend thoroughly.

Pour batter into greased and floured 10 × 14 × 2-inch pan. Top batter with reserved sugar mixture, crushed almond brickle, and almonds. Bake at 350°F for 30 minutes or until done. Serve cake warm.

almond raisin nut cake

candy cake

A unique way to serve the chocolates you receive for the holidays.

Yield: 12 servings

> **1 recipe Milk-Chocolate Icing**
> **(recipe follows)**
> **2 9-inch chocolate-cake layers**
> **12 assorted chocolates**

Prepare Milk-Chocolate Icing as directed. Spread frosting between cake layers; stack layers. Frost top and sides of cake; smooth surface with frosting knife.

Arrange chocolates on top of cake to indicate serving pieces.

Do not refrigerate, as the temperature change will discolor the chocolates.

milk-chocolate icing

Yield: Approximately 2 cups

> **½ cup butter**
> **1 pound powdered sugar, sifted**
> **¼ cup milk**
> **1 small plain milk-chocolate bar,**
> **melted**

Cream butter until smooth. Beat in sugar, a small amount at a time, beating well after each addition. Add milk and chocolate; beat until icing becomes light and fluffy.

funny-face cupcakes

Yield: 10 cupcakes

> **1 1-layer yellow-cake mix**
> **1 recipe Cream-Cheese Frosting (see**
> **Index)**
> **10 chocolate-mint wafers**

Prepare cake mix as directed. Fill cupcake papers ⅔ full. Bake for 15 to 20 minutes or until done. Cool.

Prepare Cream-Cheese Frosting. Reserve ¼ cup frosting; use remainder to frost cupcakes.

With reserved frosting, form happy faces on the chocolate-mint wafers. Decorate each cupcake with a frosted mint wafer.

picture on opposite page: candy cake

peanut-brittle layers

A novel way to use leftover Christmas candy.

Yield: 12 servings

**1 cup Peanut-Butter Cream-Cheese
Frosting (see Index)
2 9-inch spice-cake layers
2 cups crushed peanut brittle
10 to 12 assorted-shaped pieces
peanut brittle
3 cups whipped topping**

Spread Peanut-Butter Frosting between cake layers. Frost sides and top of cake with 2 cups whipped topping, being sure sides and top are frosted smooth. Cover sides of cake with crushed peanut brittle, by lightly pressing peanut brittle against sides of cake with palms of your hands. Arrange pieces of peanut brittle randomly on top of cake, flat-side-down.

Using a pastry tube and a plain tip, pipe whipped topping between candy pieces. Form a rippled edge of whipped topping around top edge of cake, using a pastry tube and serrated ribbon tip. Refrigerate.

chocolate-chip angel cake

An interesting way to decorate a cake for someone who does not care for frosting.

Yield: 12 servings

**1 angel-food cake mix
½ cup chocolate chips, chopped
fine
1 quart hand-dipped vanilla ice
cream
1 cup hot-fudge sauce**

Prepare cake mix as directed. Fold in chocolate chips. Bake as directed. Cool. Slice into serving pieces.

Spoon ice cream into serving dish; place in center of large serving tray. Arrange cake slices around ice cream.

Heat hot-fudge sauce. Serve with cake and ice cream.

sugar-plum cake

A child's dream.

Yield: 12 servings

2 9-inch yellow-cake layers
2 cups whipped cream
1 cup toasted almonds
Gum drops
Candied fruit

Frost cake layers with whipped cream, being sure sides and top are covered.
Place small amount of whipping cream in an icing bag. Using a rosette tip, pipe
rosettes in a circle on top of cake, as illustrated. Decorate each whipped-cream
rosette with a gum drop or with candied fruit. Refrigerate until ready to serve.

sugar-plum cake

vegetable-garden cake

Marzipan candy carrots add an interesting color contrast to the white frosting and powdered-sugar dust.

Yield: 10 servings

3 eggs, beaten until fluffy
1 cup oil
2 cups granulated sugar
1½ cups shredded zucchini packed tightly
½ cup shredded carrots, packed tightly
2 cups all-purpose flour
1 teaspoon salt
2 teaspoons baking soda
½ teaspoon baking powder
1 teaspoon vanilla
½ cup ground almonds
½ teaspoon cinnamon
1 recipe Milk Glaze II (recipe follows)
½ cup powdered sugar, sifted
10 marzipan carrots

Combine beaten eggs, oil, and sugar; mix well. Stir in zucchini and carrots. Add remaining ingredients as listed, up to Milk Glaze; stir until well-moistened.

Pour batter into 2 greased and floured 9-inch cake pans. Bake at 350°F for 25 to 30 minutes or until done. Cool slightly before removing from pans. Freeze 1 cake layer for use at another time.

Prepare Milk Glaze as directed. Cover top of cake generously with glaze. Place small amount of glaze on a teaspoon; drizzle glaze in a scalloped design around the edges, as illustrated.

Dust top of cake with powdered sugar. Arrange marzipan carrots around outer edge of cake.

milk glaze II

Yield: Approximately ¾ cup

2 cups powdered sugar, sifted
2 to 3 tablespoons canned milk
1 teaspoon vanilla

Combine ingredients; beat until smooth.

picture on opposite page:
vegetable-garden cake

blueberry-jam cake

Yield: 8 servings

1 8-inch yellow-cake layer
1 cup blueberry jam
1 teaspoon grated lemon rind
½ cup powdered sugar

Prepare and bake cake. Remove from pan; cool. Slice in half horizontally.
Combine blueberry jam with grated lemon rind; mix well. Spread evenly on top of bottom cake layer. Top with remaining cake layer. Dust top of cake with powdered sugar.

double-jam rolls

An easy dessert to dress up Sunday dinner.

Yield: 16 servings

1 angel-food cake mix
1 cup powdered sugar

2 cups apricot jam
2 cups strawberry jam

Prepare cake mix as directed. Pour batter into 2 waxed-paper-lined jelly-roll pans. Spread out dough evenly. Bake in 350°F oven 15 minutes. Remove from oven; cool for 5 minutes.
Turn cakes out onto a tea towel dusted with powdered sugar. Remove waxed paper. Spread cakes with jam. Roll and secure towels around rolls for 1 hour. Remove towels; slice.

porcupines

A unique way to add fruit to your child's meal.

Yield: 8 servings

1 3-ounce package cream cheese,
softened
2 to 3 tablespoons milk
1 8-inch white-cake layer

8 pear halves, drained
1 cup chocolate sprinkles
1 cup blanched almond slivers

Combine cream cheese and milk; whip until of spreading consistency. Frost top of cake with a thin layer of cream cheese.
Coat each pear half with cream cheese; sprinkle tops with chocolate sprinkles. Cover each pear with almond slivers to resemble quills. Place decorated pears on top of cake. Cut cake into serving pieces.

big foot

A treat for the Big Foot fan in your family.

Yield: 12 servings

1 2-layer devil's-food cake mix
1 recipe Chocolate Icing (recipe follows)
2 cups chocolate sprinkles
1 tube decorator's red icing

Prepare cake mix as directed. Pour into greased and floured 13 x 9 x 2-inch oblong pan. Bake at 350°F for 35 to 40 minutes or until done. Cool; remove from pan.
Prepare Chocolate Icing.
Enlarge a Big Foot print so it will measure 12 inches long by 9 inches wide. Place pattern on cooled cake; cut out pattern.
Frost cake footprint with Chocolate Icing; sprinkle top with chocolate sprinkles. Outline toenails on foot; fill in with red decorator's icing.

chocolate icing

Yield: Approximately 2 cups

½ cup margarine
1 pound powdered sugar, sifted
4 tablespoons milk
1 ounce pre-melted chocolate

Cream margarine until smooth. Beat in powdered sugar, ½ cup at a time, beating well after each addition. Beat in milk and chocolate until icing becomes light and fluffy.

whipped cream and whipped topping

Whipped cream and whipped topping can be used interchangeably in recipes, providing a few guidelines are followed:

1) It takes approximately 1½ cups of whipped topping to equal 1 cup of whipped cream.
2) One-half cup of whipping cream will expand to 1 cup of whipped cream.
3) Whipped topping will hold up better when other ingredients are added.
4) Whipped topping will last longer as a cake covering if it is not served immediately.
5) When either of these cake coverings is used, the cake must be kept refrigerated.

animal cakes

If you own one of those popular animal cake pans on the market, here is another method to use in decorating these cakes.

Yield: 16 servings

1 baked animal cake
3 to 4 cups whipped topping
Appropriate food coloring
Candies or raisins for facial
**   features**

Prepare and bake cake as directed. Remove from pan; cool completely.

Tint whipped topping the appropriate colors as indicated in the frosting directions for the cake.

Cover cake generously with colored topping. Form facial features, using candies or raisins. Refrigerate until ready to serve.

banana-split cake

A treat for the banana-split gourmet.

Yield: 12 servings

1 9-inch chocolate-cake layer
1 quart strawberry ice cream,
    softened
1 quart vanilla ice cream,
    softened

1 cup pineapple sundae topping
2 cups whipped cream
2 cups chopped mixed nuts
12 whole maraschino cherries with
    stems

Using a sharp knife or a string, slice cake into 3 layers.

Spread ice cream into 2 9-inch cake pans, using 1 quart of ice cream per pan. Freeze until hardened.

Layer the cake with the ice-cream layers, starting and ending with a cake layer. Fasten cake and ice-cream layers together by spreading ¼ cup pineapple topping between each layer.

Frost top and sides of cake with whipped cream. Sprinkle chopped nuts on top and sides of cake.

Form 12 rosettes on top of cake to indicate serving pieces. Place a cherry in the center of each rosette. Freeze cake until ready to serve.

chocolate mint roll

A different flavor treat for your next bridge luncheon.

Yield: 8 servings

3 cups whipped topping
1 teaspoon mint flavoring
2 to 3 drops green food coloring
30 chocolate wafers
2 tablespoons crème de menthe

Combine whipped topping, mint flavoring, and green food coloring; mix well. Spread each wafer generously with whipped topping; stack 5 deep. Chill for 30 minutes.

Stand stacks on serving plate to make one long roll. Frost outside with re-maining whipped topping. Freeze roll at least 1 hour before serving.

To serve, drizzle crème de menthe over frosted roll. Slice diagonally at a 45° angle.

bing-cherry delight

Yield: 12 servings

1 package black-cherry gelatin
1 cup sweetened bing cherries, pitted
1 quart vanilla ice cream, softened
1¼ cups vanilla-wafer crumbs
6 tablespoons butter, melted

1 cup powdered sugar
2 tablespoons cherry juice
2 cups whipped cream
12 whole canned bing cherries, pitted

Prepare black-cherry gelatin as directed. Stir in bing cherries. Pour into a 9-inch cake pan. Chill until firm.

Mold ice cream in a 9-inch cake pan; chill until firm.

Combine cookie crumbs and butter. Work until all crumbs are moistened. Divide crumbs into 3 equal parts.

Just prior to serving, assemble cake in the following manner:

Spread ⅓ of crumb mixture on a serving platter. Unmold gelatin; place on top of crumb mixture on serving platter. Spread second portion of crumbs on top of gelatin. Unmold ice cream; place on top of crumb-topped gelatin. Spread remaining crumbs on top of ice cream.

Combine powdered sugar and cherry juice; stir until smooth. Pour over top layer of crumbs.

Frost sides of cake with whipped cream. Score top of cake to indicate serving pieces. Decorate each piece with a whipped-cream rosette and bing cherry.

fresh-strawberry angel delight

Yield: 8 servings

1 10-inch-round prepared angel-food cake
1 cup whipped cream
1 cup cut-up fresh strawberries
1 cup whole fresh strawberries

Cut angel-food cake in half horizontally. Spread ½ cup whipped cream over bottom half of cake; sprinkle cut-up strawberries over whipped cream. Replace top half of cake; frost top with remaining whipped cream. Arrange whole strawberries on top of cake. Refrigerate until ready to serve.

picture on following pages: bing-cherry delight

chocolate refrigerator cake

Yield: 8 servings

2 cups whipping cream
¼ cup sugar
1 teaspoon vanilla
30 chocolate-nut wafers

Whip cream until peaks form. Fold in sugar and vanilla; whip until stiff.

Spread each wafer generously with whipped cream; stack 5 deep. Chill for 30 minutes.

Stand stacks on serving plate to make one long roll. Frost outside with remaining whipped cream. Freeze roll at least 1 hour before serving.

To serve, cut roll diagonally at a 45° angle.

fudge and cream layers

Yield: 2-layer 9-inch cake

4 ounces unsweetened chocolate
½ cup boiling water
2 cups granulated sugar
2 cups all-purpose white flour
1 teaspoon baking soda
1 teaspoon salt
½ cup margarine
3 eggs
⅔ cup milk
2 teaspoons vanilla
1 pint whipping cream

Shave chocolate into double boiler; cover with boiling water; stir until chocolate melts and mixture thickens. Add ½ cup sugar. Cook and stir for 2 minutes longer. Cool to lukewarm.

Combine flour, baking soda, and salt.

Cream margarine and 1¼ cups sugar until light and fluffy. Add eggs, one at a time, beating thoroughly after each addition. Add dry ingredients alternately with milk, starting and ending with dry ingredients, beating after each addition to blend. Add 1 teaspoon vanilla, then the chocolate mixture; blend.

Pour batter into 2 greased and floured 9-inch pans. Bake in 350°F oven 30 minutes or until cake has pulled away from sides of pan. Cool.

Whip whipping cream until stiff. Fold in ¼ cup sugar and 1 teaspoon vanilla.

Using a thread and a gentle sawing motion, or using a sharp, thin knife, cut each layer in two. Spread whipped cream between layers and over top and sides. Chill until serving time.

hazelnut layer

Yield: 12 servings

½ pint whipping cream
¼ cup granulated sugar
1 teaspoon vanilla
½ cup ground hazelnuts
1 9-inch white-cake layer
12 whole hazelnuts

Whip cream until it starts to hold its shape. Continue to beat while gradually adding sugar and vanilla. Fold in ground hazelnuts.

Spread whipped cream smoothly over cake layer. Mark serving pieces in topping. Garnish each serving piece with a whipped-cream rosette and a whole hazelnut. Refrigerate.

hazelnut layer

lemon cream layer

For a change, try lemon pudding and whipped cream for a cake frosting.

Yield: 8 servings

1¼ cups granulated sugar
¼ cup cornstarch
1 cup water
1 egg, beaten
2 tablespoons butter
⅓ cup lemon juice

1½ teaspoons vanilla
1 9-inch yellow-cake layer
½ pint whipping cream
½ cup chopped pecans
1 dozen candied cherry halves

Mix 1 cup sugar and cornstarch in top of double boiler. Gradually add water. Cook over boiling water until mixture thickens. Gradually add ½ of hot mixture to beaten egg. Add back to remaining filling in top of double boiler; cook for an additional 3 minutes. Remove from heat. Stir in butter, lemon juice, and ½ teaspoon vanilla. Cool for 5 minutes.

Pour pudding into shallow dish; cover with waxed paper. Refrigerate until set.

Hollow out approximately a 1-inch circle from the center of the cake layer, leaving a 1½- to 2-inch rim around the edge.

Stir chilled pudding until smooth. Fill hollowed-out cake with pudding until pudding flows over the sides.

Whip cream until it begins to hold its shape. Gradually add ¼ cup sugar and 1 teaspoon vanilla while beating. Continue to beat until soft peaks form in the cream.

Spread whipped cream over pudding, starting with a mound of cream in the center and tapering cream out to sides of cake.

Sprinkle pecans and cherries over whipped cream. Refrigerate.

peaches and cream cake

Yield: 12 servings

1 8-inch angel-food tube cake
1 cup fresh sliced peaches
2 cups vanilla ice cream, softened
3 cups whipping topping

Slice 1 inch off top of cake; hollow out center of cake, leaving a 1½-inch border around edge and a 2-inch bottom layer. (Use center pieces for Fondue — see Index.) Layer sliced peaches and softened ice cream in hollowed-out center. Replace top.

Frost top and sides of cake with whipped topping. Form swirls in whipped topping with the back of a tablespoon. Freeze cake at least 1 hour before serving.

chocolate-covered pear layer

Yield: 12 servings

10 canned pear halves, drained
1 9-inch yellow-cake layer
½ cup corn syrup
¼ cup hot water
¼ cup butter
1 12-ounce package chocolate
    chips
1 can pressurized whipped
    topping

Slice each pear half into 3 equal slices. Arrange sliced pears in a circle around outer edge of cake layer.

Combine corn syrup, hot water, and butter in saucepan. Heat to boiling. Remove from heat; stir in chocolate chips until well-blended. Cool to warm.

Cover cake with warm glaze. Let glaze set before decorating with whipped topping, as illustrated.

chocolate wheel

Yield: 12 servings

2 ounces premelted unsweetened
    chocolate
⅓ cup powdered sugar
2 cups whipped topping
2 9-inch devil's-food
    chocolate-cake layers
1 cup chopped almonds

Fold chocolate and powdered sugar into whipped topping until evenly distributed.

Spread chocolate topping evenly over top of one cake layer; sprinkle with ½ cup almonds. Place second cake layer on top of frosted layer; cover top with remaining whipped topping. Swirl the whipped topping with the back of a cold tablespoon. Sprinkle remaining nuts over swirls.

quick orange nut layers

Yield: 8 servings

½ cup whipping cream
2 tablespoons granulated sugar
1 teaspoon grated orange rind
2 8-inch purchased dessert layers
1 cup chopped pecans

Whip cream until stiff. Blend in sugar and orange rind.
Spread whipped cream between the dessert layers and over tops and sides.
Sprinkle tops with chopped pecans. Chill until serving time.

whipped-cream torte

Yield: 12 servings

10 egg whites
1⅓ cups sugar
2 teaspoons vanilla
1⅓ cups finely ground blanched
    almonds
10 egg yolks
½ cup sugar
¼ teaspoon salt
1 cup margarine
3 cups whipped cream
12 fresh raspberries
1 cup toasted almonds

Beat egg whites until stiff but not dry. Beat in 1⅓ cups sugar, a small amount at a time. Beat in 1 teaspoon vanilla. Fold in ground almonds. Pour into 2 greased and floured 10-inch cake pans. Bake at 325°F for 50 minutes. Cool; remove from pans.

Place egg yolks in top of double boiler; beat vigorously over boiling water until creamy. Stir in ½ cup sugar and salt. Remove from heat; cool.

Cream margarine until soft; stir into egg mixture. Mix in vanilla.

Spread cooled filling between torte layers. Spread whipped cream on sides and top of torte. Decorate top with whipped-cream rosettes. Top each rosette with a whole raspberry. Press almonds onto sides of torte. Refrigerate.

ribbon loaf

Yield: 10 servings

> 1 15-ounce gingerbread mix
> 8 ounces cream cheese, softened
> 1 cup whipping cream
> 2 teaspoons vanilla
> ½ cup chopped pecans
> ¾ cup finely chopped dates
> ¼ cup granulated sugar

Prepare and bake gingerbread in loaf pan as directed. Remove from pan; cool.

Combine cream cheese and ⅓ cup whipping cream; mix until smooth. Stir in 1 teaspoon vanilla, pecans, and dates.

Slice gingerbread into 3 layers. Spread cream-cheese mixture between layers. Wrap filled cake in plastic wrap. Refrigerate for 2 hours.

Whip ⅔ cup cream until it forms soft peaks. Add sugar and 1 teaspoon vanilla while beating. Continue beating until whipped cream holds its shape.

Slice cake into serving pieces; place on serving plates. Top each slice with a mound of whipped cream.

tic-tac-toe cake

If you have trouble dividing a cake evenly, this is a clever way to cut perfect serving sizes.

Yield: 9 servings

> 1 8-inch-square white-cake layer
> 1½ cups whipped topping
> 3 tablespoons melted semisweet
>   chocolate
> 2 to 3 drops red food coloring
> 2 to 3 drops green food coloring

Frost top and sides of cake layer with 1 cup whipped topping. Divide cake into 9 equal pieces, forming the game board. Form grooves in the topping on the lines used to form the game board; drizzle chocolate into these grooves.

Divide remaining whipped topping in half; color each half with a different food coloring. Form Xs and circles on the game board. Fill circles with green whipped topping and Xs with red whipped topping.

strawberry–chocolate ice-cream torte

Yield: 12 servings

1 8-inch chocolate-cake layer
2 quarts strawberry ice cream,
    softened
3 cups whipped topping
12 whole strawberries

Using a sharp knife or a string, slice cake into 3 layers.

Spread ice cream into 2 8-inch cake pans, using 1 quart ice cream per pan. Freeze until hard.

Layer cake with ice-cream layers, starting and ending with a cake layer. Fasten layers together with small amount of whipped topping. Spread whipped topping over top and sides of cake. Mark serving sizes on top of cake.

Form a whipped-topping rosette on each serving piece; top with a strawberry. Return cake to freezer to set ice cream. Keep frozen.

strawberries and cream cake

Yield: 10 servings

1 package strawberry gelatin
1 cup boiling water
½ cup cold water
1 cup frozen sweetened
    strawberries
2 cups whipped cream
12 whole strawberries

Dissolve gelatin in boiling water. Stir in cold water and 1 cup strawberries. Pour gelatin into shallow 1-quart round bowl; chill until firm.

Unmold gelatin onto serving plate. Frost outside of gelatin cake with 1¼ cups whipped cream. Evenly space 11 strawberries around bottom edge of frosted cake. Put remaining whipped cream in pastry tube. Using a serrated ribbon tube, form pillars between strawberries. Top cake with remaining strawberry.

strawberry layer

An attractive way to serve the fruits of labor from your strawberry patch.

Yield: 8 servings

½ pint whipping cream
¼ cup sugar
1 teaspoon rum
1 9-inch white-cake layer
2 cups strawberry halves

Whip cream until stiff. Fold in sugar and rum. Spread generously over top and sides of cake layer. Refrigerate.

Just prior to serving, arrange strawberries in circles over top of cake.

strawberry layer

violet garden

A springtime treat for your next bridge-club luncheon.

Yield: 8 servings

1 8-ounce spice-cake mix
5 to 6 drops green food coloring
1 9-ounce container whipped
   topping
2 dozen crystallized violets

Prepare cake mix as directed. Bake in 1½-quart greased and floured oven-proof mixing bowl at 350°F for 30 minutes or until done. Remove from bowl; cool.

Fold food coloring into whipped topping until topping is evenly tinted.

Fill pastry bag with whipped topping. Using a rosette tip, cover cooled cake with whipped-topping rosettes, as illustrated. Arrange crystal violets randomly over frosted cake. Refrigerate at least 2 hours to set before serving.

violet garden

meringue

Meringue is generally associated with baked Alaska, in which a sheet cake is topped with frozen ice cream, then coated with meringue, and baked at a very high temperature for a short period of time.

As you page through this meringue chapter, you will find other decorative uses of meringue for you to try.

To make successful meringue, you should start with room-temperature egg whites and a grease-free glass bowl and beaters. Plastic bowls tend to give poor results in making meringue, because oil tends to cling to the plastic material, thus reducing the volume of the finished meringue.

baked alaska

A simple yet elegant dessert.

Yield: 18 servings

1 8-ounce yellow-cake mix
8 egg whites
¼ teaspoon cream of tartar
½ cup granulated sugar
½ gallon cherry–nut ice cream
Spring flowers

Prepare cake mix as directed. Pour batter into greased 9-inch-square cake pan. Bake as directed. Remove from pan; cool.

Beat egg whites until foamy. Add cream of tartar; mix in. Add sugar gradually, continuing to beat until egg whites form stiff peaks.

Remove ice cream from container; round ice-cream corners. Place ice cream on top of cake layer. Cover ice cream and cake generously with meringue, being sure to smooth entire surface.

Fill pastry bag with meringue. Using a rosette tip, decorate baked Alaska as illustrated. Place in preheated 400°F oven 3 minutes or until meringue just begins to turn brown.

Decorate with spring flowers. Serve immediately.

angel almond layer

Yield: 12 servings

1 package angel-food cake mix
1 cup strawberry jam
8 egg whites
¼ teaspoon cream of tartar
½ cup granulated sugar
¼ cup thinly sliced almonds

Prepare angel-food cake mix as directed. Pour into loaf angel-food cake pan. Bake as directed. Invert pan; cool. Remove cake from pan. Cut cake in half horizontally; spread jam between layers.

Whip egg whites until foamy. Gradually beat in cream of tartar and sugar until egg whites stand in peaks.

Spread meringue on sides and top of cake. Sprinkle almonds over top of meringue. Bake in 450°F oven 3 minutes or until meringue starts to turn light brown.

angel almond layer

blueberry torte

Yield: 12 servings

4 egg whites
¼ teaspoon salt
¼ teaspoon cream of tartar
1¾ cups granulated sugar
2 tablespoons cornstarch
⅔ cup blueberry juice

1 tablespoon margarine
2 tablespoons honey
1½ cups frozen blueberries
½ cup whipping cream
1 teaspoon vanilla

Beat egg whites until frothy. Sprinkle salt and cream of tartar over egg whites; continue beating until peaks form. Add 1 cup sugar gradually; continue to beat until very stiff, dry peaks form.

Draw an 8-inch circle in the center of a brown paper; place on cookie sheet. Spread meringue ½ inch thick in the circle. Build up the sides with remaining meringue. Place in preheated 450°F oven; shut off heat. Leave in oven overnight. (Do not open oven door during this period.)

Combine ½ cup sugar and cornstarch. Add blueberry juice. Cook, stirring constantly, until thick and clear. Stir in margarine, honey, and blueberries. Chill. Pour into meringue shell; chill at least 6 hours before serving.

Combine whipping cream, vanilla, and ¼ cup sugar; whip until stiff. Cover blueberries just prior to serving.

chocolate-meringue tower

Yield: 12 servings

1 2-layer chocolate-cake mix
1 teaspoon cinnamon
½ cup raisins
½ cup walnuts

4 egg whites
1⅓ tablespoons cocoa
⅓ cup granulated sugar
¼ cup strawberry jam

Reserve ¼ cup cake-mix powder for later use. Combine remaining cake-mix powder and cinnamon. Add rest of ingredients called for in cake mix; mix batter as directed.

Dust raisins and nuts with reserved cake mix; stir into cake batter. Pour batter into greased and floured 9-inch cake pans. Bake as directed. Remove from pans; cool.

Whip egg whites until foamy. Gradually add cocoa and sugar; beat until egg whites stand in stiff peaks.

Spread jam between cake layers; stack layers. Cover top and sides of cake with meringue in a swirl design. Bake in 400°F oven 3 minutes or until meringue sets. Be careful not to burn it.

ruby ring around

Yield: 12 servings

1 9-inch white-cake layer	¼ cup granulated sugar
4 egg whites	1 cup fresh cranberries
1 teaspoon cream of tartar	

Hollow a 1-inch center from cake layer.

Beat egg whites until foamy. Gradually add cream of tartar and sugar; continue to beat until meringue stands in stiff peaks. Reserve ¾ cup meringue for rippled topping. Fill center of cake with meringue; sprinkle top with cranberries.

Fill pastry bag with remaining meringue. Using a ripple-edged tip, form a circular meringue ribbon, as illustrated.

Bake in 400°F oven 4 minutes or until meringue begins to turn light brown.

ruby ring around

snowcap mary anns

Yield: 8 servings

2 cups sliced fresh strawberries	4 egg whites
½ cup granulated sugar	¼ teaspoon salt
8 Mary Ann shells	

Combine strawberries and sugar. Fill Mary Ann shells with ¼ cup sweetened strawberries.

Whip egg whites until stiff. Gradually beat in 1 cup sugar and salt until egg whites stand in peaks.

Cover strawberries with meringue. Bake in 400°F oven 4 minutes or until meringue turns light brown.

strawberry snowballs

These simple desserts can be made ahead of time and frozen until ready for use.

Yield: 8 servings

6 egg whites
⅓ cup granulated sugar
1 quart strawberry ice cream
8 shortcake shells

Beat egg whites until stiff. Add sugar gradually; continue to beat until meringue stands in peaks.

Place ½-cup scoop of ice cream in center of each shell. Cover ice cream and cake completely with meringue.

Bake in 450°F oven about 4 minutes or until meringue starts to turn light brown. Serve immediately.

pear meringue cake

Yield: 12 servings

½ cup shortening
¼ cup brown sugar
1 egg, beaten
1 cup flour
⅓ cup finely chopped pecans
2 teaspoons dried lemon peel
1 egg white, slightly beaten
¼ cup strawberry jam
9 canned pear halves
4 egg whites
⅓ cup sugar

Cream together shortening and brown sugar. Beat in egg. Add flour, nuts, and lemon peel; mix well. Press dough on bottom of 8 × 8 × 2-inch cake pan. Brush top with 1 beaten egg white.

Bake crust in 350°F oven 15 minutes or until golden brown. Cool. Spread cooled crust with strawberry jam. Top with pear halves, rounded-side-up.

Beat 4 egg whites until stiff. Add sugar gradually; continue to beat until peaks form and will stand alone. Pile meringue in swirls on top of pears. Bake in 400°F oven until meringue is light brown.

queen of hearts crown

100

meringue squares

Yield: 16 servings

1 8-ounce white-cake mix (1 layer)
8 egg whites
½ cup granulated sugar
1 quart chocolate ice cream

Prepare cake mix as directed. Pour into square 8-inch pan. Bake as directed. Cool.

Beat egg whites until stiff. Add sugar gradually; continue to beat until meringue stands in peaks.

Cut cooled cake into 16 2-inch squares. Place a scoop of ice cream (about ¼ cup) in center of each square; frost outside with meringue. Bake in 450°F oven about 4 minutes or until meringue turns light brown. Serve immediately.

queen of hearts crown

An elegant dessert to dress up a simple meal.

Yield: 12 servings

4 egg whites
¼ teaspoon cream of tartar
Dash of salt
¼ cup granulated sugar
1 9-inch white-cake layer
½ cup toasted almonds
1 cup cherry pie filling

Whip egg whites until stiff. Gradually beat in cream of tartar, salt, and granulated sugar until egg whites stand in peaks.

Spread sides of cake with meringue. Cover with toasted almonds.

Spread cherry pie filling on top of cake to within 1 inch from edge of cake.

Fill pastry bag with meringue. Using large rosette tip, form a double row of meringue rosettes around edge of cake.

Bake in preheated 425°F oven 4 minutes or until tips of meringue turn brown, as illustrated.

strawberry meringue flan

The flan pan gives this cake its decorative border.

Yield: 8 servings

1 1-layer yellow-cake mix
2 egg whites
Dash of salt

2 tablespoons granulated sugar
1 cup frozen strawberries,
  thawed

Prepare cake mix as directed.

Grease and flour an 8-inch flan pan. Pour cake batter into pan. Bake as directed. Remove cake from pan; cool. Place cake top-side-down on baking tray.

Whip egg whites until foamy. Add salt and sugar gradually; continue to beat until egg whites stand in stiff peaks.

Pour thawed strawberries into center of cake. Cover with meringue. Bake in 450°F oven 2 to 3 minutes or until meringue begins to turn light brown. Serve immediately.

coconut-cream torte

Yield: 12 servings

4 egg whites
¼ teaspoon salt
¼ teaspoon cream of tartar
2 cups granulated sugar
8 egg yolks
½ cup flour

2½ cups low-fat milk
1½ teaspoons pure vanilla
  extract
3 tablespoons margarine
1 cup flaked coconut
¼ cup toasted coconut

Beat egg whites until frothy. Sprinkle salt and cream of tartar over egg whites; continue beating until peaks form. Add 1 cup sugar gradually; continue to beat until very stiff, dry peaks form.

Draw an 8-inch circle in the center of a brown paper; place on a cookie sheet. Spread meringue ½ inch thick in the circle. Build up the sides with remaining meringue. Place in preheated 450°F oven; shut off heat. Leave meringue in oven overnight. (Do not open oven door during this period.)

Combine egg yolks, 1 cup sugar, and flour in large mixing bowl; beat until creamy.

Heat the milk in top of double boiler just to boiling point. Slowly add heated milk to egg mixture, stirring constantly to prevent curdling. Return pudding mixture to double boiler; continue to cook until mixture coats a wooden spoon, about 8 to 10 minutes. Add vanilla, flaked coconut, and margarine; continue to cook until mixture thickens.

Cool filling to lukewarm before pouring into baked meringue shell. Sprinkle top with toasted coconut; chill torte until firm. Serve this the same day.

raspberry angel fluff

Yield: 12 servings

½ cup butter, melted
½ cup liquid brown sugar
1 2-layer yellow-cake mix
1½ cups strawberry pie filling
4 egg whites
¼ cup granulated sugar
¼ teaspoon cream of tartar

Combine butter and brown sugar. Divide evenly between 2 greased 9-inch cake pans.

Prepare cake mix as directed. Divide evenly between the 2 prepared cake pans. Bake as directed. Cool cake 5 minutes; invert on cooling racks. Wait another 5 minutes before removing pans.

Place 1 inverted cake layer on baking sheet covered with heavy brown paper. Spread pie filling evenly over this layer. Top with remaining layer.

Whip egg whites until foamy. Gradually beat in sugar and cream of tartar until egg whites stand in peaks.

Spread meringue on top of cake. Bake in 400°F oven about 4 to 5 minutes or until meringue turns light brown. Serve immediately.

raspberry angel fluff

special-occasion cakes

peppermint lane

A special birthday cake for a friend or family member when you must travel with the cake.

Yield: 1 13 × 9-inch sheet cake

2¼ cups cake flour
1½ cups sugar
3 teaspoons baking powder
1 teaspoon salt
⅔ cup shortening
1 cup milk
1 teaspoon peppermint flavoring
3 eggs
⅔ cup chopped pecans
2 cups whipped topping
2 to 3 drops red food coloring
⅓ cup crushed peppermint candy

Combine 2 cups flour, sugar, baking powder, and salt. Add shortening and ⅔ cup milk. Beat with mixer at medium speed 2 minutes, scraping bowl constantly. Add remaining milk, flavoring, and eggs. Beat for 2 minutes more. (Batter will be thinner than regular cake batter.)

Dust nuts with ¼ cup flour; fold into cake batter. Pour batter into greased and floured 13 × 9-inch oblong pan. Bake cake at 350°F for 40 to 45 minutes. Cool cake in pan.

Color whipped topping with red food coloring to desired tint. Fold in crushed peppermint candy; spread over cooled sheet cake. Refrigerate.

party cone cakes

A child-pleasing treat for a birthday party.

Yield: 24 cupcake cones

1 2-layer white-cake mix
24 flat-bottom ice-cream cones
1 recipe Fluffy White Frosting
(see Index)
2 to 3 drops red food coloring
½ cup candy beads

Prepare cake mix as directed on package. Fill cones ⅔ full of cake batter. Bake as directed for cupcakes. (Place cones in muffin tins to bake.) Cool.

Prepare frosting as directed; tint pink with red food coloring.

Hold ice-cream cone at bottom; swirl top in frosting. Sprinkle with candy.

almond dream

A delicious birthday cake for an almond-lover.

Yield: 1 9-inch 2-layer cake

1 18.5-ounce white-cake mix
2 teaspoons almond flavoring
1 pint whipping cream
¼ cup granulated sugar
Fresh red raspberries
2 cups toasted slivered almonds

Prepare cake mix as directed, adding 1 teaspoon almond flavoring with liquid called for in cake mix. Bake as directed. Cool.

Whip cream until stiff peaks form. Blend in granulated sugar and 1 teaspoon almond flavoring. Spread whipped cream between layers and over top and sides of cake.

Decorate top of cake with whipped-cream flowers. Top each flower with a red raspberry. Coat sides of cake with toasted almonds. Chill until ready to serve.

over-30 birthday cake

A novel birthday cake for those who wish to hide their true age.

Yield: 12 servings

**1 recipe Fluffy White Frosting (see
    Index)**
1 9-inch-round angel-food cake
**1 2-inch-diameter 12-inch-tall
    candle**
1 cup multicolored sprinkles

Prepare frosting mix as directed. Frost top and sides of cake. Insert a candle in center of cake. Fill in any remaining space with frosting. Sprinkle candy over top and sides of cake.

almond dream

106

birthday layers

A simple yet elegant masterpiece. If you do not own a birthday platter that will hold candles, you can use a flat platter and fasten small candle holders made with icing to the rim of the plate. Let icing set before inserting candles.

Yield: 12 servings

2 9-inch white-cake layers
4 cups powdered sugar, sifted
¼ cup hot milk
1 tube pink decorator's icing

Slice cake layers in half, using a sharp knife or a string.

Combine powdered sugar and hot milk; mix until smooth. Spread a thin layer of icing between cake layers. Spread remaining icing over edges and top of cake. Let icing set before decorating.

Using a small heart cookie cutter, evenly space heart designs around edge of cake. Using the decorator's icing, fill in heart outlines with icing. Write the desired age in center of cake. Place on serving platter. Arrange candles around outside of cake.

birthday layers

dragon fly cake

Yield: 12 servings

2 8-inch chocolate-cake layers
1 recipe Fluffy White Frosting (see
   Index)
2 cups shredded coconut
1 12-ounce package chocolate chips

Spread ¼ cup frosting between layers. Frost top and sides of cake with remaining frosting. Sprinkle coconut over top and sides of cake.

Melt chocolate chips over a double boiler. Beat with a wooden spoon to form a smooth mixture.

Trace the dragon fly pattern onto a piece of waxed paper. Make an icing bag out of greaseproof paper and cut a small hole in the end of the icing bag. Fill bag with melted chocolate. Form dragon fly by squeezing icing bag and drizzling chocolate around and around the dragon fly cut out. Layer the chocolate on the body portion to make it solid. Chill.

Lift the dragon fly parts from the waxed paper and build the dragon fly on top of the cake. If you wish to give your dragon fly dimension, place him on a mound of frosting.

dragon fly cake

sweetheart cake

sweetheart cake

Yield: 12 servings
  ½ cup margarine
  2 cups sugar
  3 egg yolks
  2 cups all-purpose flour
  3 teaspoons baking powder
  1 cup milk
  1 teaspoon vanilla
  3 egg whites, stiffly beaten
  1 recipe Fluffy White Frosting
     (see Index)
  1 cup flaked coconut
  1 teaspoon milk
  2 to 3 drops red food coloring

Cream margarine and sugar until light and fluffy. Beat in egg yolks.

Combine flour and baking powder. Add to creamed mixture alternately with 1 cup milk, beating well after each addition. Stir in vanilla.

Pour batter into 2 greased and floured heart-shaped pans. Bake at 350°F for 35 minutes or until done. Cool; remove from pans.

Prepare frosting as directed. Frost cake.

Pour coconut, 1 teaspoon milk, and red food coloring into small jar. Close jar; shake vigorously to tint coconut. Decorate outer edge of cake with tinted coconut, as illustrated.

lincoln log cake

You will need 4 15¾-ounce cans to bake this cake.. Vacuum-packed corn and pineapple are packed in this size can.

Yield: 8 servings

2 8-ounce packages devil's-food
    cake mix
1 recipe Coffee-Cream Frosting
    (see index)
1 large marshmallow

¼ cup chocolate chips
12 to 15 Chocolate Curls
    (recipe follows)
1 small tube red decorator's icing
¼ cup powdered sugar

Prepare cake mixes as directed.

Grease and flour 4 15¾-ounce cans. Fill cans approximately ½ full. Bake cakes about 20 minutes at 350°F. Cool slightly; remove from cans.

Prepare Coffee-Cream Frosting.

Slice rounded tops from cakes; lay end-to-end on flat surface. Fasten together with frosting. Cover outer surface of cake generously with frosting. Run a dinner fork over surface of cake to form the bark. Using a toothpick, draw a continuous circle on the edges, to resemble the growth layers of a log. Place the marshmallow on top of cake. Frost and decorate the stump as illustrated. Place on serving platter. Sprinkle chocolate chips randomly over cake. Arrange Chocolate Curls around log. Using the decorator's icing, draw a design on the log, as illustrated.

Prior to serving, dust serving platter with powdered sugar.

chocolate curls

Yield: Approximately 4 dozen

1 6-ounce package semisweet
    chocolate chips
1 marble slab or 1 quart
    crushed ice in large plastic
    sealable bag

Soften chocolate chips over double boiler.

Beat vigorously until they run in a steady stream from a spoon.

Pour chocolate onto a chilled marble slab or a kitchen counter chilled by using a bag of crushed ice. Spread chocolate to about ⅛ inch thick; let harden until chocolate loses its gloss, approximately 2 hours.

Using a long, slender knife, form curls by holding the knife at a slight angle and pulling it across the surface of the chocolate.

george washington's cherry cake I

An attractive cake in honor of the father of our country.

Yield: 12 servings

1 9-inch round angel-food cake
1 cup cherry preserves
1 recipe Fluffy White Frosting
  (see Index)
16 whole maraschino cherries with
  stems
16 citron slivers

Cut cake in half horizontally. Spread cherry preserves between layers.
Prepare frosting. Cover sides and top of filled cake.
Drain cherries on paper towel. Arrange cherries in clusters of 2, having stems touching at top. Form leaves around stems with slivers of citron.

lincoln log cake

george washington's cherry cake II

Yield: 1 2-layer 9-inch cake

½ cup cherry jam
2 baked 9-inch yellow-cake layers
1 recipe Fluffy White Frosting
(see Index)

Green crystal sugar
Red crystal sugar

Spread cherry jam on top of 1 9-inch cake layer. Top with remaining layer. Prepare frosting as directed. Frost stacked layers.

Draw a picture of cherries on a stem. Transfer design to waxed paper; cut out design. Carefully place the waxed paper with the cutout design on top of frosted cake. Sprinkle green crystals over stem area and red crystals over cherry area of design, being sure to cover all areas. Carefully remove waxed paper.

st. patrick's day cakes

Yield: 10 cupcakes

1 8-ounce white-cake mix
2 to 3 drops green food coloring
½ recipe Fluffy White Frosting
(see Index)

40 green candied almonds
Green food coloring

Prepare cake mix as directed. Color batter with green food coloring. Divide dough evenly among 10 cupcake papers. Bake for 15 to 20 minutes or until done. Cool.

Prepare frosting as directed. Frost cupcakes.

Using candied almonds, make a shamrock design on each cupcake. Dip a toothpick in green cake coloring; form a stem for the shamrock.

st. pat treats

Yield: 8 servings

1 8-ounce white-cake mix
2 to 3 drops green food coloring
1 quart vanilla ice cream

1 cup marshmallow cream
½ cup crème de menthe

Prepare cake mix as directed, stirring in green food coloring prior to pouring batter into pan. Pour batter into 8-inch cake pan. Bake as directed. Cool cake; remove from pan.

Soften ice cream; spread evenly over an 8-inch cake pan. Freeze until firm.

Soften marshmallow cream; spread on top of cooled cake.

Unmold ice cream; place on top of marshmallow cream. Return cake to freezer for 30 minutes to set cake.

To serve, slice cake into 8 portions. Top each portion with 1 tablespoon crème de menthe.

easter bunny cookie-cutter cake

Yield: 12 servings

2 cups powdered sugar, sifted
2 tablespoons hot milk
1 teaspoon vanilla
2 9-inch chocolate-cake layers

Combine powdered sugar, hot milk, and vanilla. Mix until smooth and free from lumps. Spread ¼ cup icing between cake layers.

Place rabbit cookie cutter in center of top of cake. Spoon icing over top of cake; let it drizzle down sides of cake. Remove cookie cutter; form rabbit's eye with a dot of frosting. Let frosting set before serving.

easter bunny cookie-cutter cake

easter-egg cakes

If your family does not like the traditional Easter eggs, try these for a surprise from the Easter Bunny.

Yield: 1½ dozen

½ cup soft butter
¾ cup powdered sugar
2 tablespoons vanilla
Dash of salt
1½ cups all-purpose flour
2 to 3 drops yellow food coloring
¼ cup chopped English walnuts
1 recipe Cream-Cheese Frosting
    (see Index)
½ cup chocolate sprinkles
½ cup multicolored sprinkles
1 cup coconut
1 teaspoon milk
2 to 3 drops green food coloring

Cream butter and sugar. Add vanilla and salt; mix in. Work in flour with your fingers. Measure out ¼ of dough; set aside. Work yellow food coloring and nuts into the remaining dough. Take approximately 1 level teaspoon of dough; form round balls. Refrigerate balls 1 hour.

While centers are chilling, divide remaining dough into 1-tablespoon portions. Remove chilled centers from refrigerator; wrap with proportioned tablespoon portions. Using your palms, roll dough to resemble shape of eggs. Place on ungreased cookie sheet. Bake eggs at 375°F for 12 minutes. Cool.

Prepare frosting as directed. Frost cooled cakes. Cover generously with sprinkles.

Place coconut in a jar.

Combine milk and food coloring; pour over coconut. Shake until coconut is evenly tinted. Arrange tinted coconut on serving platter. Scatter eggs on coconut to resemble an Easter-egg nest.

maypole centerpiece

Yield: 10 servings

1 1-layer white-cake mix
1 recipe Seven-Minute Frosting
(see Index)
3 cups shredded coconut
3 teaspoons water
2 to 3 drops green food coloring
2 to 3 drops red food coloring
2 to 3 drops yellow food coloring
2 yards ½-inch white ribbon

Prepare cake mix as directed. Divide dough evenly among 10 greased and floured muffin tins. Bake at 350°F for 15 to 20 minutes or until done. Cool; remove from tins.

Prepare frosting. Frost cupcakes generously on all sides. Divide frosted cupcakes into 3 groups.

Divide coconut evenly among 3 pint jars. Mix each food color with 1 teaspoon water; pour 1 color over each jar of coconut. Seal jars; shake until coconut is evenly tinted.

Roll each group of frosted cupcakes in a different-colored coconut.

Turn a stemmed cake stand upside down on a 20-inch square of cardboard covered with foil.

Divide ribbon into 9 equal lengths. Tape each length individually from the bottom of the stand.

Space 9 cupcakes evenly around outer rim of cake plate. Gently press a ribbon into top of each cupcake. Place the tenth cupcake on top of inverted stem so it covers where ribbons are attached to stand.

Combine remaining coconut; spread over exposed foil.

halloween cake

Yield: 12 servings

3 large ripe bananas
2 9-inch chocolate-cake layers
1¾ cups whipped topping
½ cup chocolate chips
¼ cup butter
1 egg, beaten frothy
8 peanut-butter chips
4 pieces maraschino cherries
6 orange-marshmallow cat faces
4 wooden picks

Slice 1 banana; place on top of 1 cake layer. Cover bananas with ¼ cup whipped topping. Top with remaining cake layer. Cover sides of cake with whipped topping. Refrigerate.

Combine chocolate chips and butter in saucepan; stir over boiling water until smooth. Stir chocolate mixture into frothy egg; beat until smooth. Chill until spreading consistency. Spread chocolate glaze over top of cake.

Just prior to serving, halve the 2 remaining bananas. Insert a wooden stick in cut side of each banana. Cover bananas with remaining whipped topping. Use peanut-butter chips to form eyes and cherry pieces as mouths. Insert on top of cake. Place cat faces evenly around sides of cake. Fasten with toothpicks if necessary. Refrigerate.

jack-o-lantern cake

Yield: 12 servings

1 recipe Chocolate Icing (see
    Index)
2 to 3 drops yellow food coloring
1 to 2 drops red food coloring
2 9-inch chocolate-cake layers

Prepare Chocolate Icing. Before adding the chocolate, reserve 1 cup of frosting. To reserved frosting add yellow and red food coloring to obtain a bright-orange frosting.

Frost top of 1 cake layer with chocolate frosting. Place remaining layer on top of first layer.

Outline a pumpkin on top of unfrosted layer. Cover this area with orange frosting. Using a knife, swirl the ridges of a pumpkin shell in the frosting. Frost sides and remaining top with Chocolate Icing. Draw a jack-o-lantern face on the pumpkin; fill the outline by using a toothpick dipped in chocolate icing.

thanksgiving cake

Yield: 12 servings

½ cup margarine
2 cups sugar
3 egg yolks
2 cups all-purpose flour
3 teaspoons baking powder
1 cup milk
1 teaspoon vanilla
3 egg whites, stiffly beaten
1 recipe Cooked Frosting (recipe
    follows)
½ cup chopped pecans
½ cup chopped maraschino
    cherries
Assorted marzipan fruits

Cream margarine and sugar. Add egg yolks one at a time; beat well after each addition.

Combine flour and baking powder; add to creamed mixture alternately with milk and vanilla, mixing well after each addition. Fold in egg whites.

Pour batter into 2 greased and floured 9-inch cake pans. Bake at 350°F for 30 to 35 minutes or until done. Cool in pan 10 minutes. Remove from pan.

Prepare Cooked Frosting. To ¾ cup icing, add chopped pecans and cherries; mix well. Spread between cake layers. Frost sides and top of cake with remaining frosting.

Arrange marzipan fruit around outer edge of frosted cake.

cooked frosting

Yield: Approximately 2½ cups

5 tablespoons all-purpose flour
1 cup milk
1 cup margarine
1 cup granulated sugar
1 teaspoon vanilla

Blend flour with ¼ cup milk to form a smooth paste. Add remaining milk to paste; cook until a stiff paste forms. Cool until cold.

Cream margarine and sugar. Add to paste; blend. Add vanilla; beat until frosting takes on appearance of whipped cream.

german christmas cake

Yield: 2 dozen bars

1 cup chopped English walnuts
½ cup chopped candied fruit
¼ teaspoon dried orange peel
1¾ cups flour
½ teaspoon baking soda
½ teaspoon salt
½ teaspoon ground cloves
½ teaspoon nutmeg
1 teaspoon cinnamon
½ cup butter
¼ cup brown sugar, packed
1 egg, beaten
⅓ cup honey
1 recipe Rum Glaze
     (recipe follows)
24 red cherry halves
120 whole blanched almonds
24 citron slivers

Mix walnuts, candied fruit, and orange peel.

Combine flour, baking soda, salt, and spices; sprinkle over fruit and nut mixture.

Cream butter and brown sugar until fluffy. Beat in egg. Add honey alternately with flour and nut mixture; mix well.

Spread batter onto greased jelly-roll pan. Bake in preheated 375°F oven 15 minutes or until done. Remove cake from oven. Frost with Rum Glaze.

Score top of cake into serving portions. Decorate each portion with a flower, using the cherry halves as centers, surrounded by petals made from whole almonds and stems formed from citron slivers. Slice when cool.

rum glaze

Yield: Approximately ¾ cup

¼ cup water
1 cup powdered sugar
1 teaspoon rum flavoring

Combine ingredients; beat until smooth.

date nut star

A delicious and different way to serve a holiday cake.

Yield: 12 servings

2½ cups all-purpose white flour
4 teaspoons baking powder
1 teaspoon salt
1 cup granulated sugar
⅓ cup butter
1 cup ale
1 egg, beaten
½ cup chopped walnuts
1 cup finely chopped dates
1 recipe Cream-Cheese Frosting
  (recipe follows)
¼ cup slivered almonds
¼ cup English-walnut halves
¼ cup cashews
1 whole red candied cherry
Silver sprinkles

date nut star

Combine flour, baking powder, salt, and sugar. Cut in butter until mixture resembles a coarse meal. Form a "well" in center of dry ingredients. Add ale and egg; mix just until all flour mixture is dampened. Stir in walnuts and dates.

Turn mixture into well-greased star mold. Spread mixture to sides of pan, leaving center slightly hollowed. Bake cake in 350°F oven 1 hour or until done. Remove from pan; cool.

Frost top of cake with Cream-Cheese Frosting. Decorate with remaining ingredients, as illustrated.

cream-cheese frosting

Yield: 1 cup

3 ounces cream cheese, softened
2 tablespoons butter
½ teaspoon vanilla flavoring
1¾ cups powdered sugar

Beat cream cheese, butter, and vanilla until smooth. Gradually add sugar; beat until fluffy.

christmas cutout cake

An easy way for a busy mother to add holiday trimming to her Christmas-Eve dessert.

Yield: 10 servings

**Cutouts from Christmas cards or
    coloring book
1 9-inch chocolate-cake layer
1 cup powdered sugar, sifted**

Cut out holiday figures to fit the dimensions of the cake. Arrange these figures on top of cake layer in an attractive design. Dust top of cake with sifted powdered sugar. Remove cutout designs. Cover cake until serving time, to prevent dryness.

christmas cutout cake

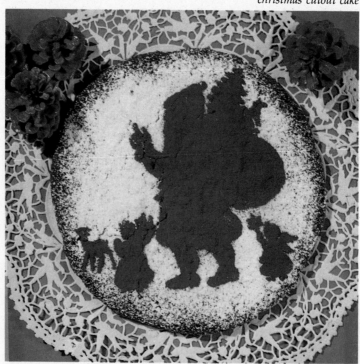

rudolph's portrait

To make this cake, you will need a lamb cake mold.

Yield: 10 servings

1 cup granulated sugar
½ cup shortening
¾ cup milk
1½ teaspoons vanilla
2 cups all-purpose flour
2 teaspoons baking powder
2 egg whites, stiffly beaten

2 cups whipped topping
1 ounce premelted chocolate
1 maraschino cherry
1 small marshmallow
2 small twigs
1 cup flaked coconut

Cream sugar and shortening until light and fluffy.

Combine milk and vanilla.

Sift together flour and baking powder. Add alternately with milk mixture to creamed sugar and butter. Beat well after each addition. Fold in beaten egg whites.

Grease and flour lamb mold. Pour batter into face part of mold. Insert a small wooden toothpick in the nose for support; cover with other half of mold, being sure to lock the edges.

Place mold on baking sheet. Bake cake at 375°F for 45 minutes. Cool cake for 10 minutes, turn mold on back half, and remove face half. Remove cake from back half.

Combine 1¾ cups whipped topping and premelted chocolate; mix until well-blended. Frost cake with chocolate topping.

Using the ¼ cup reserved white topping, form a white breastplate and white tail on the deer. Form Rudolph's nose with the cherry.

Cut the small marshmallow in half; form Rudolph's eyes. Place twigs above the ears to form antlers.

Place cake on serving platter. Surround with flaked coconut. Refrigerate.

christmas snowballs

A quick and easy dessert for a Christmas buffet.

Yield: 12 servings

12 purchased snowball cakes
12 small red or green birthday
    candles
24 small green plastic leaves

Place snowballs on dessert plate. Insert a candle in center of each snowball. Place a leaf on either side of each candle.

When ready to serve, dim the lights, and light the candles.

cupcake wreaths

Use these holiday treats when you must transport a large number of desserts to a holiday gathering.

Yield: 30 cupcakes

1 2-layer white-cake mix
1 recipe Cheese Frosting (recipe follows)

2 to 3 drops green food coloring
1 to 2 drops red food coloring

Prepare and bake cake mix as directed for cupcakes, filling each cupcake about ⅔ full. Cool.

Prepare frosting; reserve 1½ cups. Frost cupcakes with remaining frosting. Let frosting set for 24 hours.

Tint 1 cup reserved frosting with green food coloring. Using a serrated ribbon tube, circle outer edges of frosted tops to resemble Christmas wreaths.

Tint remaining ½ cup frosting with red food coloring. Using a drop flower tube, place a small flower at bottom of Christmas wreath.

cheese frosting

Yield: Approximately 3 cups

1 8-ounce package cream cheese, softened
⅓ cup butter

1 teaspoon vanilla
1 pound powdered sugar, sifted

Beat cream cheese, butter, and vanilla until smooth. Gradually add sugar; beat until fluffy.

christmas-tree cake

A Christmas-Eve treat for the kids.

Yield: 12 servings

1 baked 13 × 9-inch sheet cake
3 cups whipped topping
2 to 3 drops green food coloring

½ cup flaked coconut
Assorted miniature gum drops

Using a coloring book cutout of a Christmas tree as a pattern, cut a Christmas tree from the sheet cake.

Tint whipped topping with green food coloring. Frost cutout cake with tinted whipped topping, being sure to cover all cut sides.

Using coconut, string a garland down frosted Christmas tree. Decorate tree with gum drops. Refrigerate.

new year's clock

Use this ice-cream cake as the perfect ending to your New Year's party.

Yield: 32 servings

1 gallon vanilla ice cream
3 cups hot-fudge sauce
1 small tube green decorator's
    icing
2 cups chopped walnuts

Purchase ice cream in an ice-cream store. Request that they cut the gallon of ice cream from a 5-gallon serving container, or pack ice cream in a 2-gallon round Dutch oven. Freeze ice cream 24 hours to harden.

Remove ice cream from container. If it will not come out of container, cover outside of container with a wet towel for a few minutes.

Place ice cream on serving platter. Smooth top and sides with a warm, damp knife.

Spoon hot-fudge sauce (do not heat) into a pastry tube. Using a serrated ribbon tube, form a decorative edge around top edge of ice-cream cake.

Change pastry-tube tip to a plain round tube. Form a clock's face on top of cake.

Using small tube of decorator's icing, write "Happy New Year" on top of cake.

Press chopped nuts around sides of cake. Return cake to freezer.

Remove cake from refrigerator ½ hour before serving. Cut with a warm, wet knife.

Note: If cake is stored in a frost-free freezer, cover with an aluminum tent to prevent freezer burn.

chocolate rose dream

Yield: 12 servings

**2 9-inch-square chocolate-cake
   layers
1 recipe Coffee-Cream Frosting
   (recipe follows)
25-30 chocolate leaves (see Index)**

Spread ¼ cup frosting between layers. Frost top and sides of cake with a light cover of frosting.

Place star tip in icing bag and fill with frosting. Cover top and sides of cake with icing stars. (To obtain straight rows, draw lines in frosting prior to decorating.)

Starting from the outside and working towards the center, build a chocolate rose in the center of the frosted cake.

coffee-cream frosting

Yield: Approximately 3 cups

**2 teaspoons freeze-dried coffee
¼ cup boiling water
½ cup margarine
½ cup shortening
5 cups powdered sugar, sifted
1 egg, beaten**

Dissolve coffee in boiling water; reserve.

Cream margarine and shortening until fluffy. Beat in 2½ cups sugar until smooth. Add egg; mix well. Add remaining sugar; continue to beat until frosting is well-mixed and free from lumps. Add coffee; beat until frosting becomes light and fluffy.

chocolate rose dream

cream-cheese flower layers

Yield: 12 servings

½ cup margarine	1 teaspoon baking soda
1 cup brown sugar	½ cup sour cream
1 cup granulated sugar	2 cups all-purpose flour
3 egg yolks	3 egg whites, beaten stiffly
½ cup strong coffee, hot	2 batches Cream-Cheese
⅓ cup cocoa	Frosting (see Index)

Cream margarine and sugars until light and fluffy. Add egg yolks; beat until batter is thick.

Gradually add coffee to cocoa; let stand until cooled. Add to butter and sugar mixture.

Dissolve soda in cream. Add alternately to sugar mixture with flour, beating well after each addition. Fold in beaten egg whites.

Pour batter into 2 well-greased and floured 9-inch cake pans. Bake in 350°F oven 35 to 40 minutes or until done. Remove from pans; cool.

Prepare frosting as directed. Spread frosting between cake layers; stack layers. Spread frosting over sides and top of cake. Score top of cake to indicate serving pieces.

Using a ribbon-edge piping tip and frosting-filled pastry bag, form a flower on each serving piece, as illustrated.

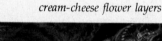

cream-cheese flower layers

springtime festival

A kitchen masterpiece to welcome in the season of spring.

Yield: 1 3-layer 9-inch cake

1½ cups vegetable oil	3 large carrots, grated
2 cups sugar	½ cup chopped walnuts
¼ cup hot water	5 egg whites, beaten stiff
5 egg yolks	1 recipe Fluffy White Frosting
2½ cups all-purpose flour	(see Index)
2 teaspoons cinnamon	5 carrot curls
1½ teaspoons baking soda	5 orange-rind strips
½ teaspoon salt	Fresh flowers

Combine vegetable oil, sugar, hot water, and egg yolks; beat on low speed until well-blended.

Combine 2¼ cups flour, cinnamon, baking soda, and salt in large bowl. Add egg-yolk mixture alternately with carrots to dry ingredients, blending well after each addition.

Combine remaining ¼ cup flour and walnuts, being sure nutmeats are thoroughly coated with flour. Fold nuts and beaten egg whites into cake batter.

Pour batter into 3 well-greased and floured 9-inch cake pans. Bake in 300°F oven 1 hour or until done. Cool; remove from pans.

Prepare frosting as directed. Frost tops of each layer; stack to form 3 tiers. Garnish top tier with flowers made by cutting thin carrot curls into petals and using orange-peel strips to form stems.

Place cake on serving platter. Prior to serving, arrange fresh cut flowers around base of cake.

lemon ginger packages

Yield: 10 servings

1 15-ounce gingerbread mix	1 recipe Fluffy White Frosting
1½ cups milk	(see index)
1 package lemon pudding mix	2 to 3 drops yellow food coloring

Prepare gingerbread mix according to package directions. Pour mixture into greased and floured 9-inch-square pan. Bake at 350°F for 40 to 45 minutes or until done. Cool.

Add milk to pudding mix; cook over low heat until thickened. Cool.

Using a sharp knife or a thread, divide gingerbread into 3 layers. Spread pudding between layers; divide into 10 bars.

Prepare frosting as directed. Using ½ of Fluffy White Frosting recipe, frost tops and sides of each bar.

Tint remaining frosting with yellow food coloring. Using a pastry tube, decorate frosted bars with flowers and bows.

orange rosette cake

A showcase for one who has mastered the art of cake decorating.

Yield: 8 servings

⅓ cup margarine
⅓ cup butter
1¾ cups sugar
2 eggs
1½ teaspoons orange extract
3 cups all-purpose flour

½ teaspoon salt
3 teaspoons baking powder
1¼ cups milk
1 recipe Orange Butter-Cream
    Frosting (see Index)

Cream together margarine, butter, and sugar until fluffy. Add eggs, 1 at a time, beating well after each addition. Stir in orange flavoring.

Sift flour, salt, and baking powder together. Add to creamed mixture alternately with milk, beating well after each addition.

Pour batter into 2 9-inch greased and floured cake pans. Bake in 350°F oven 35 minutes or until done. Cool; remove from pans.

Prepare Orange Butter-Cream Frosting.

Freeze one cake layer for use at another time. Place remaining layer, bottom-side-up, on a flat plate. Spread top and sides evenly with frosting, being sure frosting is spread smooth. Refrigerate for 1 hour to set frosting.

Fill icing bag fitted with a plain round tube with frosting. Form lattice design on top of cake. Place a dot of frosting where the lines cross.

Change tip on icing bag to a small rosette tube. Decorate sides of cake as illustrated. Refrigerate for 1 hour prior to serving, to set frosting.

fluffy white frosting

A successful cooked frosting depends on *all* the ingredients being at room temperature, and on following the directions.

Yield: Approximately 4 cups

2 egg whites
¾ cup granulated sugar
⅓ cup light corn syrup

2 tablespoons warm water
¼ teaspoon salt

Combine all ingredients in 4-quart ovenproof glass mixing bowl. Beat for 1 minute on high with an electric mixer. Place bowl over boiling water. (Be sure the bottom of the bowl does not touch the metal of the pan with the boiling water.) Beat for *exactly* 7 minutes. Remove from boiling water; beat until frosting stands in peaks.

Note: Coloring or flavoring may be added after frosting is removed from boiling water.

orange butter-cream frosting

Yield: Approximately 3 cups

1 cup butter, softened
5 cups powdered sugar, sifted
1 egg, beaten

2 tablespoons orange-juice concentrate
1 to 2 drops red food coloring
2 to 3 drops yellow food coloring

Cream butter until light and fluffy. Add 2½ cups sifted powdered sugar; beat vigorously until smooth. Add beaten egg; mix well. Beat in remaining powdered sugar. Pour in orange juice and food coloring, beating until frosting becomes fluffy.

orange rosette cake

spiderweb cake

Yield: 12 servings

1 2-layer yellow-cake mix
1 cup apricot jam
4 cups powdered sugar
¼ cup hot milk

1 teaspoon vanilla
1 ounce semisweet chocolate
1 teaspoon butter

Prepare cake mix as directed. Pour into 3 greased and floured 9-inch cake pans. Bake as directed. Remove from pans; cool.

Heat jam until it will spread easily. Spread jam between cake layers; stack layers.

Combine powdered sugar, hot milk, and vanilla; beat until smooth. Spread icing over cake.

Melt chocolate and butter over double boiler; stir until well-blended.

Make circles or lines on top of cake. With a string or sharp knife make 8 evenly spaced strokes toward edge of cake. To make the web, make 8 additional upward strokes toward the center between the 8 original strokes, as illustrated.

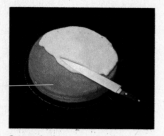

Spread icing over cake.

Make chocolate lines on top of cake.

Make 8 evenly spaced strokes toward edge of cake.

spiderweb cake

lemon coconut cake

A light dessert for a backyard picnic.

Yield: 1 2-layer 9-inch cake

> 1 18.5-ounce white-cake mix
> 1 tablespoon grated lemon rind
> 1 package lemon pudding mix
> 1½ cups milk
> 1 recipe White-Cloud Icing (recipe
>   follows)
> 1 cup coconut

Prepare cake mix as directed, adding grated lemon rind with the liquid ingredients. Bake cake in 2 9-inch layer pans as directed on package. Cool; remove from pans.

Prepare lemon pudding, using 1½ cups milk. Cool. Spread lemon pudding over top of 1 layer of cake; top with remaining cake layer.

Frost tops and sides of cake with White-Cloud Icing. Sprinkle coconut over sides and top of frosted cake.

white-cloud icing

Yield: 1½ cups

> 1½ cups granulated sugar
> ⅓ cup water
> 2 egg whites
> ¼ teaspoon salt
> ⅛ teaspoon cream of tartar

Combine ingredients in top of double boiler; beat for 1 minute. Place over boiling water; beat until mixture forms peaks and is stiff enough to spread.

rose cake

Yield: 12 servings

**2 recipes Basic Royal Icing (see
    Index)
Red coloring
Blue coloring
Yellow coloring
2 9-inch white cake layers**

Prepare icing recipes. Tint one frosting recipe pink using approximately 8 parts red to 1 part blue coloring. Spread ¼ cup frosting between cake layers. Stack layers and frost top and sides of cake. Let set to harden.

Using ⅓ of white frosting recipe, decorate sides of cake in the following manner:

Attach rose tube to icing bag and pipe ruffle on the side of the cake.

Using the star tube, pipe shell border around the bottom and top borders of the cake. Let cake set to harden icing.

Divide remaining icing into 5 parts and color as follows:

Yellow—use yellow coloring

Red—use red coloring

Orange—use yellow and red coloring

Blue—use blue coloring

Green—use yellow and blue coloring

Pipe 1 large rose and 2 small roses of each color with the exception of green. Let set to harden.

Arrange the four large flowers in the center of the cake. Attach with icing.

Attach corresponding small roses on top border of cake as shown. Attach with icing.

Using the leaf tube, pipe leaves between roses to create a balanced design. Let set to harden before serving.

bridal basket

Yield: 12 servings

**2 recipes Basic Royal Icing (see
    Index)**
Red and blue food coloring
2 8-inch white-cake layers
Marzipan Roses (see Index)

Prepare icing, leaving one recipe white. Color remaining recipe pink by mixing blue and red food coloring to obtain the desired shade. (approximately 8 parts red food coloring to one part blue)

Spread a thin layer of pink icing between layers and stack. Ice top and sides of cake with a smooth layer of icing. Let icing set to harden.

Place a round tube in an icing bag. Fill bag with pink icing. Place pink icing vertical staves at one-inch intervals around the sides of the cake.

Place a basket weave tip in an icing bag. Fill bag with white icing and pipe wickers around side of cake as follows:

Pipe wickers over first stave, ½ inch on either side, keeping serrated edge up and leaving enough space between wickers for alternate row.

Pipe between the first set of wickers, over the second stave, ½ inch on each side. (This set of wickers will begin at the first stave, cross over the second stave and end at the next 1 inch guide line.)

Continue this process until entire cake is covered.

Form handles by wrapping 4 aluminum wires with masking tape. Bend wires to form handle and separate at the center. Attach to cake. Spread icing liberally over the handle. Let set to harden.

Form 9-10 Marzipan Roses and let harden. Arrange on top of cake. Accent with fern leaves and ribbons.

bridal basket

baking in gelatin molds

Individual metal gelatin molds are ideal for making holiday baked treats for family or friends.

A variety of these molds can generally be found in the housewares section of a department store. When selecting molds suitable for baking, remember the entire surface must be greased and floured to ensure easy removal of the cakes.

The following are four examples of how these molds can be used for baking.

christmas wreaths

Yield: 2 dozen wreaths

1 16-ounce pound-cake mix
½ cup water
½ cup mashed bananas
2 eggs
1 cup chopped candied mixed fruit
1 recipe Fluffy White Frosting
    (see Index)
2 dozen whole red and green
    candied cherries

Reserve 2 tablespoons cake-mix powder for later use. Combine remaining cake mix, water, bananas, and eggs. Mix until powder is moistened. Set mixer on medium speed; beat for 3 minutes.

Combine chopped candied fruit and reserved cake mix; mix thoroughly. Fold into cake batter.

Fill greased and floured individual ring molds ⅔ full. Bake in 325°F oven 20 minutes or until done. Remove from pan to cool.

Prepare Fluffy White Frosting as directed. Frost wreaths, being sure to cover tops and sides.

Slice whole cherries; decorate frosted wreaths.

easter baskets

A unique treat for a school Easter party.

Yield: 12 servings

1 1-layer yellow-cake mix
1 recipe Mae's Seven-Minute
Frosting (recipe follows)
1 cup coconut
2 teaspoons milk
2 to 3 drops green food coloring
1 cup small jelly beans
12 pipe cleaners

Prepare cake mix as directed.
Grease and flour individual gelatin ring molds. Fill molds ½ full of dough. Bake at 350°F for 20 minutes or until done. Remove from pans; cool.
Prepare frosting. Frost cakes.
Put coconut, milk, and food coloring into a jar; shake until coconut is colored evenly. Fill centers of frosted cakes with tinted coconut topped with jelly beans. Form basket handles with pipe cleaners.

mae's seven-minute frosting

This recipe makes enough frosting to cover a 1-layer cake.

Yield: Approximately 1 cup

1 egg white
¾ cup + 2 tablespoons granulated
sugar
3 tablespoons cold water
½ teaspoon vanilla

Combine egg white, sugar, and water in top of double boiler. Place over rapidly boiling water; beat at high speed exactly 7 minutes. Remove from heat. Add ½ teaspoon vanilla; continue to beat until frosting is of spreading consistency.

chocolate easter bunnies

These chocolate bunnies will delight the hearts of both young and old at Easter time.

Yield: 8 to 10 rabbits

1 8-ounce chocolate-cake mix
1 cup coconut
2 to 3 drops green food coloring
½ cup jelly beans, assorted colors

Prepare cake mix as directed. Fill greased and floured individual molds ⅔ full (approximately ¼ cup batter). Bake at 350°F for 15 to 20 minutes or until done. Unmold; cool.

Tint coconut with green food coloring. Arrange on serving platter.

Place chocolate bunnies on green coconut bed. Scatter jelly beans among rabbits. Cover with plastic wrap until serving time, to prevent drying.

jam rings

Yield: 12 servings

1 1-layer white-cake mix
1½ cups red currant jelly
1 cup sliced peaches, well-drained
1 can pressurized whipped
**   topping**
½ cup toasted almonds

Prepare cake mix as directed.

Grease and flour miniature ring molds. Fill molds ½ full of dough. Bake at 350°F for 20 minutes or until done. Remove from pans; cool.

Heat jelly; drizzle over cake rings.

Arrange 3 or 4 peach slices inside each ring. Top with whipped topping and almonds.

quick dress-up cakes

With the busy life-styles of today, many of us would enjoy serving a fancy decorated cake for dessert, "if we only had the time."

With the use of cake mixes, ready-made frostings, and a few decorative ingredients, beautiful cakes like those shown here can be made in a very short period of time.

cherry-cream layers

Yield: 12 servings

1 2-layer white-cake mix
1 can prepared vanilla frosting
2 to 3 tablespoons maraschino
    cherry juice
36 whole maraschino cherries

Prepare cake mix as directed. Divide dough evenly among 3 well-greased and floured 8-inch cake pans. Bake as directed. Remove from pans; cool.

Using an electric mixer, color frosting with maraschino cherry juice. Spread frosting between cake layers; stack layers. Spread remaining frosting over sides and top of cake.

Divide cake into 12 serving pieces. Decorate each piece with a cluster of 3 cherries.

vanilla-cream cake

All that is needed to decorate this cake is a pastry bag with a rosette tip.

Yield: 12 servings

1 can prepared vanilla frosting
2 9-inch white-cake layers

Spread small amount of frosting between cake layers to hold them together. Frost top and sides of cake. With a sharp knife, score 12 serving markers in icing on top of cake.

Place small amount of frosting in small pastry bag. Using rosette tip, form a rosette on each serving piece. Your cake is ready to serve.

*starting at top center
and reading clockwise:
orange chocolate layers
vanilla-cream cake
cherry-cream layers
date pistachio cake
triple chocolate cake
lemon love cake
mint cake*

date pistachio cake

Yield: 12 servings

1 2-layer white-cake mix
½ cup ground pistachios
1 can prepared vanilla frosting
1 cup chopped pistachios
1 cup dates

Prepare cake mix as directed. Divide dough evenly among 3 well-greased and floured 8-inch cake pans. Bake as directed. Remove from pans; cool.

Fold ground pistachios into frosting. Spread small amount of frosting between cake layers; stack layers. Frost top and sides of cake.

Press chopped pistachios around sides of cake. Arrange dates in a random design around outside edge of cake.

triple-chocolate cake

Yield: 12 servings

1 can prepared chocolate frosting
2 8-inch chocolate-cake layers
1 cup Chocolate Curls (see Index)

Spread small amount of frosting between cake layers; stack layers. Spread remaining frosting over sides and top of cake. Press chocolate curls around sides and rim of cake, as illustrated.

lemon love cake

Yield: 12 servings

1 2-layer lemon-cake mix   **1 tablespoon lemon juice**
1 can prepared vanilla frosting   **2 drops yellow food coloring**

Prepare cake mix as directed. Pour into 3 well-greased and floured 8-inch cake pans. Bake as directed. Remove from pans; cool.

With an electric beater combine vanilla frosting, lemon juice, and food coloring. Beat until well-blended.

Spread frosting between layers; stack layers. Spread frosting evenly over top and sides of cake. Place small amount of frosting in pastry bag. Using ribbon-edge tip, form a curled ribbon design around edge of cake.

mint cake

Yield: 12 servings

1 can prepared vanilla frosting
½ teaspoon mint flavoring
2 to 3 drops green food coloring
¼ cup crushed green after-dinner
    mints

2 8-inch white-cake layers
12 fresh mint sprigs

Combine frosting, mint flavoring, and green food coloring. Beat with an electric mixer until well-blended. Fold in crushed mints.

Spread frosting between cake layers; stack layers. Spread remaining frosting over top and sides of cake. Score cake into 12 serving pieces. Decorate each piece with a mint sprig.

orange chocolate layers

Yield: 12 servings

1 teaspoon dried orange peel
1 2-layer white-cake mix
1 can prepared chocolate frosting

2 tablespoons grated orange peel
12 pecan clusters
Strips of dried orange peel

Add dried orange peel to cake powder. Prepare cake mix as directed. Pour batter into 3 well-greased and floured 8-inch cake pans. Bake as directed. Remove from pans; cool.

Frost cake layers, covering sides and top evenly. Sprinkle grated orange peel over top of cake. Decorate each serving piece with a pecan cluster and dried orange strips.

marble tower

The designs created by the marbling in the cake and the fluted pan give this cake its decorative touches.

Yield: 12 servings

1 1-layer devil's-food-cake mix
1 1-layer yellow-cake mix

Prepare each cake mix as directed.

Grease and flour a 2-quart fluted tube pan. Pour yellow-cake mix into pan; top with devil's-food batter. Run a knife through dough to marble cake. Bake in 350°F oven 40 minutes or until done. Cool for 5 minutes before removing cake from pan.

index